The Effects o G000112155 Livelihood

Berhanu Ayalew

The Effects of HIV/AIDS on Urban Livelihood

A household level analysis in Bahirdar, Ethiopia

LAP LAMBERT Academic Publishing

Impressum / Imprint

Bibliografische Information der Deutschen Nationalbibliothek: Die Deutsche Nationalbibliothek verzeichnet diese Publikation in der Deutschen Nationalbibliografie; detaillierte bibliografische Daten sind im Internet über http://dnb.d-nb.de abrufbar.

Alle in diesem Buch genannten Marken und Produktnamen unterliegen warenzeichen-, marken- oder patentrechtlichem Schutz bzw. sind Warenzeichen oder eingetragene Warenzeichen der jeweiligen Inhaber. Die Wiedergabe von Marken, Produktnamen, Gebrauchsnamen, Handelsnamen, Warenbezeichnungen u.s.w. in diesem Werk berechtigt auch ohne besondere Kennzeichnung nicht zu der Annahme, dass solche Namen im Sinne der Warenzeichen- und Markenschutzgesetzgebung als frei zu betrachten wären und daher von jedermann benutzt werden dürften.

Bibliographic information published by the Deutsche Nationalbibliothek: The Deutsche Nationalbibliothek lists this publication in the Deutsche Nationalbibliografie; detailed bibliographic data are available in the Internet at http://dnb.d-nb.de.

Any brand names and product names mentioned in this book are subject to trademark, brand or patent protection and are trademarks or registered trademarks of their respective holders. The use of brand names, product names, common names, trade names, product descriptions etc. even without a particular marking in this works is in no way to be construed to mean that such names may be regarded as unrestricted in respect of trademark and brand protection legislation and could thus be used by anyone.

Coverbild / Cover image: www.ingimage.com

Verlag / Publisher:
LAP LAMBERT Academic Publishing
ist ein Imprint der / is a trademark of
OmniScriptum GmbH & Co. KG
Heinrich-Böcking-Str. 6-8, 66121 Saarbrücken, Deutschland / Germany
Email: info@lap-publishing.com

Herstellung: siehe letzte Seite /
Printed at: see last page
ISBN: 978-3-659-52646-6

Acknowledgments

First and for most, I would like to thank the almighty God for giving me the strength to start and complete my study.

Then I would also like to extend my deepest gratitude and appreciation to my thesis advisor, Daregot Berihun (Ph.D) for his guidance at ease; comments and supervision with patience; encouragement; at all different stages of the research.

I extend special thanks to Dawn of Hope Ethiopia Charitable Association Bahir Dar Branch Staffs for their support and cooperation during data collection. I also extend my thanks to all the informants/participants in the survey and focus group discussions who gave me the necessary information without hesitation.

I am grateful to thank my Brothers Meseret Ayalew, Amsalu Ayalew and my Sisters Mastewal Ayalew, Emeneshe Ayalew. At last but not least,

I am delighted to express my worm and deepest thanks to my love Ethiopia Assaye for her precious time scarify during data gathering and entry and she rely share my feelings and find out what I want any time and any movement

1

TABLE OF CONTENTS   **PAGES**

LISTS OF TABLES   PAGES

4

LISTS OF ACRONYMS

AIDS	Acquired Immune Deficiency Syndrome
ART	Anti Retroviral Therapy
CBOs	Community Based Organizations
CCF	Christian Children Fund
CSA	Central Statistical Authority
DHS	Demography Health Survey
DoH	Dawn of Hope Ethiopia Charity Association
ECA	Economic Commission for Africa
FGD	Focus Group Discussion
FHI	Family Health International
HAPCO	HIV/AIDS Prevention and Control Office
HHH	Household head
HIV	Human Immune Deficiency Virus
HBC	Home Based Care
IGA	Income Generating Activities
MoH	Ministry of Health
MWCY	Ministry of Women, Children and Youth
PLHIV	People Living with HIV/AIDS
SSG	Self Saving Group
TB	Tuberculosis
UNAIDS	Joint United Nations Program on HIV/AIDS
WFP	World Food Program

Abstract

While there is a growing literature on HIV/AIDS in Ethiopia, the focus has been on the epidemiology. Therefore, this study tries to fill some of the information gap on the livelihood conditions of HIV infected and affected households and as such support better design of interventions. The overall objective of the study was to explore the effects of HIV/AIDS on urban household livelihood security in Bahir Dar City, Ethiopia. The study used a variant of the Sustainable Livelihood Framework (SLF) developed by the DFID to examine how HIV/AIDS affects the human, physical, financial and social capitals of urban households. Different food security indicators are also examined to assess how HIV/AIDS affects households' food security. **Mortality**: According to the findings, a total of 18 deaths were reported from all surveyed households over the 12 months preceding the survey. **Income:** The regression results shows that a unit (grade) change in household head's educational attainment changes households income by about 27%. **Asset** of households are sold to make up the lost income. **Food Security status;** a higher percentage of affected households had poor consumption score and used more severe coping strategies.

Key words; HIV/AIDS, Livelihood, Food Security, Capital, Resilience, Vulnerability,

Chapter 1: INTRODUCTION

1.1 General Background

Ten years after the landmark UN General Assembly Special Session on HIV/AIDS (UNGASS), progress was reviewed at the 2011 UN General Assembly High Level Meeting on AIDS. A new Political Declaration on HIV/AIDS with new commitments and bold new targets was adopted. The 2011 declaration builds on two previous political declarations: the 2001 Declaration of Commitment on HIV/AIDS and the 2006 Political Declaration on HIV/AIDS at UNGASS, in 2001, Member States unanimously adopted the Declaration of Commitment on HIV/AIDS. This declaration reflected global consensus on a comprehensive framework to achieve Millennium Development Goal Six-: halting and beginning to reverse the HIV epidemic by 2015 (UNDP, 2012).

It is recognized that the need for multisectoral action on a range of fronts and addressed global, regional and country-level responses to prevent new HIV infections, expand health care access and mitigate the epidemic's impact. The 2006 Political Declaration recognized the urgent need to achieve universal access to HIV treatment, prevention, care and support. While these three declarations have been adopted only by governments, their vision extends far beyond the governmental sector to private industry and labor groups, faith-based organizations, nongovernmental organizations and other civil society entities, including organizations representing people living with HIV (UNAIDS, 2012)

The emergence of the HIV epidemic is one of the biggest public health challenges the world has ever seen in recent history. In the last three decades HIV has spread rapidly and affected all sectors of society- young people and adults, men and women, and the rich and the poor. Sub-Saharan Africa is at the epicenter of the epidemic and continues to carry the full brunt of its health and socioeconomic impacts (USAID, 2012).

Since the 1980s economic shocks and socio-political changes in Africa have resulted in changes not just household livelihood strategies but also to the social relationships within and between households and families, affecting the social resources available to people for constructing secure livelihoods and protecting themselves against shocks and stresses. Economic decline and the effects of the HIV/AIDS pandemic have impoverished many and trapped large numbers in permanent poverty. Recent reviews stress the need to understand the dynamics of poverty, especially the factors that impoverish households or enable them to escape poverty, permanently or temporarily (Hulme and Shepherd, 2003).

The livelihood strategies and well-being of urban households in sub-Saharan Africa have been affected by short-term shocks and long duration stresses due to economic decline, increasing poverty, deteriorating living conditions and the HIV/AIDS epidemic. Some households are more able to adapt and recover from shocks and stresses than others. Their responses are likely to depend on the assets available to the household; their access to socioeconomic contexts (Pelling and Wisner, 2009).

The literature on the relationship of HIV/AIDS and livelihoods in general and the relationship to food security in particular has been growing fast in recent years. There is also empirical evidence on HIV/AIDS *vis a vis* its effect on food and livelihoods security from small scale studies mainly in East and Southern Africa. The evidence on the relationship of HIV/AIDS to livelihood security is diverse. Still, some livelihood security related factors that are affected by HIV/AIDS are known from research. What the diversity of the evidence demands is, in order to design appropriate interventions, context specific examination of the extent to which HIV/AIDS affects various aspects of livelihood security in a country and in specific areas with in a country is needed (UNAIDS, 2011).

Ethiopia which has a population of 86 million (UNDP, 2012), with per capita income of about US$ 392 per annum with Gini coefficient of 29.8%, is among the poorest in the world and accordingly it is ranked 174th out of 175 countries listed in UNDP's Human Development Report (2011). Over 29.6% (25.7 % urban and 33.6% rural) of the population live below the income poverty line of US$ 2 per day, with Human Development Index HDI 0.363 and 41.5%(60.5% rural and 22% urban) of the population are illiterate with 17.5% urban unemployment (UNDP 2012). Ethiopia is the third largest country in the world, with 1.3 million people living with HIV/AIDS (UNAIDS, 2012). Poverty combined with illiteracy and gender inequality aggravated the spread of HIV/AIDS in the country and results in many poor to remain livelihood insecure (CARE International, 2010).

Even though Bahir Dar city is benefiting from its natural location and being political center of the Amhara region that creates greater opportunities for its fast growth, most people of the City are facing many socioeconomic problems. The main problems are rural-urban migration and HIV/AIDs which are

11

inter related one to the other. Many youth migrate from the surrounding rural woredas to the City hopping better employment opportunities. These migrants are illiterate and cannot afford the cost of life in the City which causes them to engage in prostitution and day laborer works that aggravates the rate of HIV transmition (Amhara regional HAPCO, 2012).

As a result, More than 12,000 People living with HIV/AIDS (PLHIVs) and 9,033 Orphan vulnerable children (OVC) in the City are still remaining needy and livelihood insecure despite the efforts of the government, NGOs, CBOs to mitigate the effects of HIV/AIDS. The absence of family tie due to migrants from the surrounding rural woredas especially complicates the care and support services to the poor PLHIVs and orphan vulnerable children (Bahir Dar City HAPCO, 2012).

1.2 Statement of the Problem

According to UNAIDS, 2009 annual report, Ethiopia is among the countries most affected by HIV and AIDS. The existence of HIV infection in Ethiopia was recognized in the early 1980s with the first two AIDS cases reported in 1986. Since then, the epidemic has rapidly spread throughout the country. The epidemic peaked in the mid-1990s. Since 2000 the epidemic has declined in major urban areas and stabilized in rural settings.

According to projections based on the single point estimate the national adult HIV prevalence for 2009 was estimated at 2.3% with 1,116,216 People living with HIV (PLHIV) and 855,720 orphans due to AIDS. Currently, the total number of Orphan and vulnerable children (OVC) in the country is estimated at 5.4 million while prevalence decreases further to 1.5% with 800,000 PLHIV (DHS, 2011).

There were an estimated 44,751 deaths in Ethiopia due to AIDS in 2009. The number of AIDS-related deaths would have been much higher if it had not been for the free Anti retroviral Therapy (ART) program which has been scaled-up in an accelerated manner since 2005. The estimated national adult HIV incidence of 0.28% in 2009 translates to over 131,000 new HIV infections. With the current status, it is evident that HIV and AIDS remains a formidable development challenge to the country (FHAPCO, 2012).

There are a number of factors that make the nature and strength of the relationship between HIV/AIDS and livelihood security contextual. These include household demographics such as household size and composition, socio-cultural context of the community and households' access to resources (Alemtsehay and Tsedazeab, 2008).

The preparation of a multi sectoral strategy to address HIV/AIDS in Ethiopia such as "Strategic II for intensifying multisectoral HIV/AIDS Response in Ethiopia Strategic Plan Management (SPM II) (2010/11 - 2014/15)" is to be applauded. However, a lot remains to be done to understand and address the effects of HIV/AIDS on the livelihood`s of urban poor. A bibliography by Converse, *et al. (2008),* shows that studies on HIV/AIDS in Ethiopia have primarily focused on epidemiological factors with limited work on socio-economic effect of HIV.

There are few studies that look at the link between HIV/AIDS and livelihood security in Ethiopia. For example a 2004 ECA/UNDP/WFP, Alemtsehay and Tsegazeab (2008) study in 12 rural agrarian Woredas of 4 regions Amhara, Tigray, Oromya and SNNP shows that HIV/AIDS has affected livelihood in the following ways: household structure has been affected in that more single households are found among the infected and HIV/AIDS affected households divert expenditure from farming systems to non –productive items, even selling productive assets. Very few studies have been conducted on the effect of HIV/AIDS on households in Ethiopia, including the one done in 25 AIDS afflicted households (Bollinger *et al*, 1999).

However, as Garbus (2003) and Alemtsehay and Tsegazeab (2008) clearly indicated, there are no studies/researches done on the effects of HIV/AIDS on the livelihood`s and food security of existing poor Ethiopian households in urban areas and slums. Similarly, there are no studies on how the extended families are affected by the epidemic.

According to Bahir Dar City HAPCO, more than 14,000 People living with HIV/AIDS (PLHIVs) and 9,033 Orphan vulnerable children (OVC) in the city are still remaining needy and livelihood insecure despite the efforts of the government, NGOs, CBOs to mitigate the effects of HIV/AIDS and it needs detail investigation of the extent and depth of livelihood deprivation due to AIDS in order to formulate better intervention.

This study, therefore, explores and analyze how HIV/AIDS affects the livelihood`s of HIV affected households in Bahir Dar City Administration by disaggregating into the following relevant categories; changes in household capacity, capital and activities, changes in income and expenditure patterns, changes in the household and family structures and burden of dependency, situations of AIDS orphans, the link between HIV/AIDS and food security, and coping strategies.

1.3 Research Questions

The following research questions are asked in order to look for solutions for the stated problem;

- Do households affected by HIV/AIDS have access to resources and services?
- What are the sources of income for people with HIV?
- Does HIV affect the capitals of infected households?
- Does HIV/AIDS affect women more than men?
- What are the major coping strategies of HIV/AIDS affected households and individuals?
- Are HIV/AIDS affected households food secure?

1. 4 Objectives of the study

1.4.1 General Objective

The general objective of this study is to explore the effects of HIV/AIDS on household's livelihoods with a special emphasis to households affected by HIV/AIDS in Bahir Dar City, Ethiopia.

1.4.2 Specific Objectives of the study

▸ Examine how HIV/AIDS affects the human capital of urban HIV infected and affected households.

▸ Probe into the effect of HIV/AIDS on the physical capital of urban HIV affected households.

▸ Explore the linkages between HIV/AIDS and financial capital of urban HIV affected households.

▸ Assess how HIV/AIDS affects the social capital of urban HIV infected and affected households

▸ Scrutinize food security status and coping strategies of households affected by HIV/AIDS.

1.5 Significance of the Study

The household is an institution, which is the basis of any community and nation, and If AIDS affects more households, the country will face development problems. As many studies have mostly focused on demographic, psychosocial problems of PLHIVs and orphans, clinical and epidemiological problems of the epidemic, research on the nature of the problem at household level Livelihood and food security in relation to the effect of the epidemic is desirable and deserves attention. Therefore, the output of this study could be used as a record of how HIV/AIDS affected households are responding to the epidemic and the socio-economical and financial implications of the epidemic for the households and the country at large. By analyzing and indicating the real facts, it highlights areas of attentions for policy makers and NGOs working in prevention and care to draw lessons for their future intervention plans.

1.5 Limitations of the Study

As the study subjects are households drawn from beneficiaries of an NGO (Dawn of Hope Ethiopia Charitable Association) that provide care and support to HIV infected households who are referred from Hospital and Health Centers, households which are not being supported, but infected and affected by HIV/AIDS, are not included in this study.

This study is limited to the effects of HIV/AIDS on affected and infected household level livelihood and do not include the epidemiological, physiological and mental as well as prevention and control aspects of the epidemic. Due to cost and time constraints, only household heads (who are infected by the HIV virus for HIV affected households) are major respondent of all questions posted to get the whole information about their households.

1.6 Scope of the Study

Although HIV/AIDS has a wave of effects from the macroeconomic level to micro household level, this study is focusing on household level effects due to limited capacity. Within the household level analysis the study looks at the effect of HIV/AIDS on human, financial, social and physical capital as well as on food security. Also, though the relationship of HIV/AIDS and livelihood is bidirectional, the researcher has limited the study to the effect of HIV/AIDS on household livelihood and food security in order to keep the study manageable.

1.7 Operational Definitions

The following are operational definitions of terms used in this study.

Impact: A shock to an existing system of livelihood at the national, regional, communal, or household level, which reduces the levels and expectations of life and welfare. It may mean the dissolution of the unit and involve the loss of individuals from poverty related causes rather than as a direct result of HIV/AIDS illness or death (Barnett and Whiteside, 2000).

Livelihood:-the term livelihood describes the capacities, capital (human, financial, social, productive/economic, natural), and activities needed to sustain life and the ability to recover from shocks without affecting the natural resource bases (Devereux, 2002; Ellis, 2006b).

Acquired Immune Deficiency Syndrome (AIDS):- A clinical syndrome (a group of various illnesses that together characterize a disease resulting from damage to the immune system caused by infection with the human immunodeficiency virus (HIV). HIV, which causes acquired immune deficiency syndrome (AIDS), principally attacks T-4 lymphocytes, a vital part of the human immune system. As a result, the body's ability to resist opportunistic viral, bacterial, fungal, protozoa, and other infection is greatly weakened.

Poverty: Poverty is economic condition in which people lack sufficient income to obtain certain minimal levels of health services, food, housing, clothing, and education generally recognized as necessary to ensure an adequate standard of living. What is considered adequate, however, depends on the average standard of living in a particular society (Microsoft, 2002).

Households (HH): Any unit of habitual residence where some consumption and/or production may be undertaken in common and where some members may recognize culturally defined relationships of kinship and/or affinity where the members are related in some way (Barnett and Whiteside, 2000).

Gender: - refers to socially constructed roles of women and men ascribed to them on the basis of their sex. Gender roles depend on a particular socioeconomic, political and cultural context. They are learned and vary widely within and between cultures and can change (Common Wealth Secretariat, 2002).

Vulnerability- a situation when people experience high risk of events that have adverse impacts on their livelihood, and that their ability to deal with such risky events when they occur is impaired (Devereux, 2002; Ellis, 2006b)

Iddir: A community based association established on voluntary basis for the purpose of supporting each other with special attention to burial of the dead.

Equib;- informal voluntary saving among individuals to expand working capital in a revolving manner.

Infected: People infected by HIV Virus or whose blood is HIV Positive

Affected: people whose health and socioeconomic activates are affected or hindered by HIV/AIDS or develop from infected to AIDS stage.

Kebele: The smallest administrative unit under the City Administration

Sex worker: - An individual who is paid money in exchange for sex

Coping: - is about the ways in which we all recognize that our normal expectations of how life is and ought to be are adjusted when we realize that 'normality' has, for whatever reasons, switched to 'abnormality'. In recognizing that such a transition has occurred, we search for explanations of the new circumstances in which we find ourselves; we adjust our expectations and we search for courses of action that will enable us to achieve whatever goals are culturally significant for us. Is able to recover or remain resilient.

1.8 Organization of the Study

The study is organized in the following ways; **chapter one** deals with the introduction, the problem statement, research questions and objectives of the study. **Chapter two** describes the conceptual and empirical related literatures mainly focused on effects of HIV/AIDS at household, community, national and global level, and the relation between HIV/AIDS and Livelihood strategies. **Chapter three** is devoted on the methodology of the research by describing the study area, research design, sampling, data collection and analysis methods. **Chapter four** deals with findings of the study focused on human, financial, physical and social capitals as well as food security and coping strategies of the study units. And **chapter five** presents conclusions of the findings and recommendations.

Chapter 2: LITERATURE REVIEW

Several recent reviews have drawn attention to the dearth of research that investigates the impact of HIV/AIDS and the benefits of using a livelihoods approach for this purpose (White and Robinson, 2000; Seeley and Pringle, 2001; Stokes, 2003; Tobin, 2003). What work there is often focuses on a single country and the research projects do not use comparable methods. Nor does the available research analyze whether and how the impacts of economic decline and ill-health (especially HIV/AIDS) differ, in both the short and long term. The reviewers assert that policy should not be confined to improving treatment and prevention and stress the need for systematic research as a basis for interventions to mitigate the impact of HIV/AIDS and other shocks and stresses on household livelihoods.

2.1 Urban livelihood system

Vulnerability has different dimensions and can be expressed through progression at different scale and complexity. It is generally accepted that disasters do not affect all people equally. The pattern of risk is related to socioeconomic development. For instance, people with different income levels are likely to be affected differently by the same event as people's capacity to cope with them and to adapt is highly related to their living status. The vulnerability to disaster tends to lessen with increasing income as they have better capacity to cope or to adapt in ways that reduce risk. This is partly because buildings that are more expensive can be engineered to higher standard to have safer housing (Ellis, 2006b).

Higher income households are also more likely to live in areas that are less vulnerable to natural hazards and able to choose safer jobs. Besides, rich people can have assets that can be called on in emergencies and they are capable of protecting their wealth by insuring assets that are at risk. Furthermore, wealthier groups often have more influence on public expenditures to be the main beneficiaries of government investment in infrastructure and services, in the urban environment where life is highly dependent on such services (Thomas, 2008).

On the other hand, where people have great problems in meeting their daily needs, the ability to withstand disaster will be limited. This is partly because low-income groups are likely to live in areas prone to different hazards. They are always pushed to live as cheaply as possible on dangerous, marginal sites. In addition, the poorest people live in the lowest quality housing that could not withstand the magnitude of hazards.

Therefore, urbanization and poverty have serious implications for worsening conditions of housing and for the spontaneous settlements of poor people on marginal areas; and urban poverty and its associated effects make communities more vulnerable to disasters. Consequently, for millions of poor urban dwellers, managing disaster is an everyday occurrence, less noticed by outsiders. This may include the fires that wipe out squatter neighborhoods, the devastation brought by HIV, the cumulative health problems resulting from poorly ventilated shelter or the long-term effects on children of pollution. Such less noticeable disasters erode livelihoods and cost lives (Potsiou, 2010).

2.2 The Effects of HIV/AIDS on household livelihood

One of the most common shocks that impoverish poor households is illness. The most explicit and widely referred to impact of HIV/AIDS on households relates to the loss of human capital. It is argued that HIV/AIDS afflicted individuals lose their production abilities as a result of the illnesses, stress, depression and eventual death caused by the syndrome. Further loss of human capital comes by way of the household labor that is expended on caring for the afflicted household member(s). The necessity to provide such care diverts other members of the household from their daily activities, including schooling in the case of children. While all these suppositions are correct, it is

26

also true that the effects on human capital alluded to can be caused by death resulting from illnesses other than those associated with HIV/AIDS. However, given the fact that HIV/AIDS affects the most productive population cohort, its impact on household and community livelihoods is arguably more devastating than some other types of illness (Kabir et al, 2000).

2.3 Livelihood assets/capital of the urban households

Livelihood comprises the capacities, capital (human, financial, social, productive/economic, natural), and activities needed to sustain life and the ability to cope and recover from stresses without affecting the sustainable natural resources bases (Devereux, 2002).

Financial capital: This specifically refers to assets and entitlements that have a cash value. They include income; remittances from family members working away from home, sources of credit, pensions, savings and disability grant are important asset bases in the urban context.

Human capital: includes skills, knowledge, the ability to labor, education and health status of the household members and the community, and the ability to find and use information to cope, adapt, organize and innovate. As the sale of labor is important in the urban economy, health care is a crucial in determining the quality of labor. Education and training also improve the value of human capital. This form of capital is sensitive to the effect of 'everyday' risk.

Natural capital: This generally has less significance in urban context. However clean and safe local environments may be considered as an asset because health effects of the environment will have an effect on human capital.

Physical capital: This refers to housing, economic and social infrastructure and other assets (Jewelry or household goods) obtained to satisfy cultural norms and basic needs that can be sold, or pawned for cash during times of stress or low income. Although physical capital constitutes one of the most important assets in urban context, it cannot be mobilized in informal settlements where tenure rights and other legal preconditions are absent.

Social capital: Building social assets can increase the chances of greater self-reliance amongst households and neighborhoods. Social capital refers to the network of support and reciprocity that may exist within and between households and within communities, which people can call on in times of stress. However, the social context in urban areas may be characterized by crime, social fragmentation, and other social problems, which can reduce the ability of households to support one another in order to further their livelihood strategies (Johnson, 2011)

Furthermore, in urban settlements, the livelihood strategies of the poor are complex. Contexts are changing and uncertain, with rapid urban growth, increasing crime, ill-equipped public sector and intense competition for limited resources. Household members employ varied living strategies, living on credit, surviving and competing in markets. This livelihood instability can exacerbate vulnerability just as the hazard effects experienced by vulnerable populations are likely to undermine livelihoods for long (Federica Marzo, 2009)

Often a large proportion of the urban poor are forced to work in the informal sector, earning low incomes for long hours of work. Competition for work is intense, usually making incomes very low. For such workers, insurance, health care or sick pay do not exist. In addition, informal sectors are often associated with a non-dependable stream of income and precarious working conditions. Working in poor conditions serves to increase long-term vulnerability to disease and ill health. Increasingly, this is the case with child labor, where many lifelong health problems can begin (Elo, O., palm, E. and Vrolijks, 1995).

Sustainable Livelihoods Framework of poor urban people.

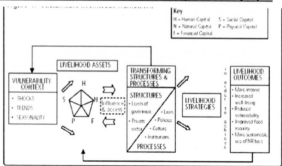

http://www.livelihoods.org/info/guidance_sheets_pdfs/section2. pdf accessed on 28 May 2013

Besides, the commoditization of urban life means that, in contrast to more rural contexts, money is required to meet even the most basic needs – water, food and shelter. Usually the poorest often pay more than their better-off neighbors do for basic services. For instance, research in Lusaka, Zambia, found that water purchased by low-income groups was nearly ten times more expensive than that from a subsequently installed water supply system. Food can also come at a high cost; and food expenditures can make up as much as 60 to 80 per cent of total expenditure amongst low-income HIV/AIDS affected households (Pelling, 2008).

There are also more *market pressures* in urban areas that cause price rises or falling incomes, and make the urban poor with inadequate incomes and limited asset bases at risk in affording accommodation, health services, as well as basic infrastructure for providing water, sanitation, drainage etc. Therefore, the urban poor are vulnerable to most environmental hazards, including most of those related to climate change such as flooding, drought. It also makes it difficult to recover from disaster, magnifying effect where the loss of accumulated assets, such as a dwelling, can set back household development irretrievably (Wisner, 2009).

In addition, poor people are not able to move, changes jobs, or have little option of finding new job if their livelihood is threatened by a disaster, as they have no saving, lack the necessary skills and educational background. At the same time, as many poor urban dwellers live on illegally occupied land so city authorities are incentivized to invest in a more resilient infrastructure (road, water, sanitation, drainage system etc) in these areas; and mostly these areas are difficult even to take emergency measures or escape when disaster occurs due to insufficient provision of public transport to evacuate. This is because government investments have largely been allocated to provide basic services to planned settlements (Smith, 2006).

Urban poverty also has negative effects on health and environmental conditions. Paradoxically, poor desperate people not only suffer from environmental decline created by rapid uncontrolled urban expansion and inadequate policies, but also themselves become a cause of ecological deterioration by over-exploiting surrounding natural resources and by neglecting environmental quality under the pressure of survival. This neglect of environmental quality may encourage the spread of diseases mainly HIV/AIDS or induce natural hazards (Petley, 2008).

2.4 Livelihood Strategies of HIV/AIDS Affected people

Death of the breadwinner has devastating effects upon families and households. Survivors suffer economically as well as emotionally. The result is shown as children become orphans, their nutrition status and health decreases, also there may be drop out of schools particularly for girls. During the illness stage, one of the first responses for those working in the informal sector is to move from directly productive activities into service oriented jobs, such as selling goods which are usually lower paid. This change allows the infected person to work when they can, as service jobs are generally less physically demanding (Gow, 2002).

Income falls, and as the illness progresses the ability to work decreases, reducing income down further. As the diseases progress the level of care required increases, creating increased demands on other members of the household. Women are especially most affected since they are particularly in developing countries responsible for domestic work and to care for the family. Thus, they are more likely to be either absent frequently or taken out of schools (Desmond, 2000).

The economic shock of a prime-age adult death is mitigated to some extent by a variety of strategies that households use to cope. According to Desmond (2000) and Gow (2002), four main coping/livelihood strategies are observed in sub-Saharan Africa. These are:

1. Doing nothing;
2. Withdrawing savings or selling assets;

3. Receiving assistance from other households; and

4. Altering household composition

2.4.1 Doing nothing

The first coping mechanism of HIV/AIDS affected households
is just to sit and see what will happen next. This is because they
have already passed through severe resource constraints by the
experience AIDS deaths. Therefore, the capacity to respond in
any meaningful way to overcome the difficulties now
confronting the household can sometimes be beyond their
capabilities. In this condition the only thing they do is to sit and
try to change nothing about their livelihood strategies.
However, in the case of Ethiopia, 'doing nothing' in most cases
is not used as a coping mechanism. But instead there are various
coping strategies such as begging, praying and using holy water
in order to be cured. A case study conducted by Demele (2004)
on 15 women living with the virus in Addis Ababa revealed that
nearly all women used religion as a primary coping strategy.

2.4.2 Dissaving and sale of assets

The second coping mechanism of households is withdrawing
savings and selling assets. HIV/AIDS affected households do
not only use their savings but they also stop saving because of
two reasons. Firstly, households make their saving choices with

respect to the perception of risk and life expectancy. If people forecast that they would not have a future, they are unlikely to save money. Secondly, people would not think about the future in such a situation where the horrible pain and suffering generated by the illness and death of a relative exists in the household. On the contrary they would let go everything they have in order to give hope or a short relief to a child or relative (USAID, 2010).

Furthermore, withdrawing savings if available and taking on more debt is usually the major options by households that struggle to pay for medical treatment or funeral costs. Then as debts mount, precious assets, such as radios, televisions, livestock and even house and land, are sold to be used as a source of income. Not only these types of assets are sold particularly in poor households, but also furniture such as cupboard, bed, as well as women's ornaments like gold necklaces are sold out. Gow and Desmond (2002) had noted that there is evidence from Tanzania and Uganda that suggests radio ownership increased in households with no deaths and decreased in households that experienced death. Once households sold their assets and used their savings, the chances of them recovering and rebuilding their livelihoods become difficult.

2.4.3 Assistance from other households

The other coping mechanism is receiving help from relatives and neighbors which is an important support to the efforts of households facing an adult death. A study conducted in Tanzania depicted that 80 to 90 percent of affected households were likely to receive assistance in cash or kind from other households (Ibid. 2002). This is only possible if the other households are relatively better off. However it is unlikely that in poor countries like Ethiopia, there are limited households which can help HIV/AIDS affected ones.

2.4.4 Altering household composition

As one or both parents die, the capacity of households to remain intact will be difficult. As a result of this relatives and friends of the family take in individual children where the resources are available to do so. Most commonly, grandparents, in particular, grandmothers seem to take over this parenting role. There may also be a situation where no able-bodied adult is available to provide resources and maintain households and families together. This leads to the dissolution of the family unit as a household being either a child headed household or displacement of children (Desmond, 2002).

A study conducted on 215 households in Zimbabwe revealed that about 40 percent of the sample households had taken in orphans who had lost both parents. And sixty five percent of households where the deceased adult female used to live before her death were reported to be no longer in existence in both the urban and rural sites (WFP, 2008). This shows that the worst effect of HIV/AIDS on households could not be seen because of the dissolution of some households, which are not possible to be counted.

But in addition to these mechanisms, some individuals and households use other mechanisms such as using holy water, begging, searching assistance from NGO, dispersing siblings, and searching assistance from community based organizations such as Iddir.

2.5 The Concept of Effects of HIV/AIDS

The effect of HIV/AIDS is multidimensional, among others the main ones are demographic, health, education, gender, orphans and elders, and effect at the household level. The most direct consequence of AIDS is an increase in mortality. According to UNAIDS, HIV/AIDS is now by far the leading cause of death particularly in sub-Saharan Africa.

In 2007 in sub-Saharan African countries estimated 2.2 million people died which is 75 percent of the three million AIDS deaths globally that year, and five million people became newly infected with HIV. HIV/AIDS reduces life expectancy of individuals. The same source indicated that in seven African countries where HIV prevalence is more than 20 percent, the average life expectancy of a person born between 2000 and 2005 is now 49 years that is 13 years lower than in the absence of AIDS. The following table depicts the average life expectancy in 11 selected African countries.

Table 2.1 Average life expectancy in 11 selected African Countries

Country	Before AIDS	After AIDS
Angola	41.3	35.0
Botswana	74.4	26.7
Ethiopia*	56.0	49.0
Lesotho	67.2	36.5
Malawi	49.4	36.9
Mozambique	42.5	27.1
Namibia	68.8	33.8
Rwanda	54.7	38.7
South Africa	68.5	36.5
Swaziland	74.6	33.0
Zambia	68.6	34.4
Zimbabwe	71.4	34.6

Source: Avert.org (2008).

As a result of all this, since the vast majority of people living with HIV/AIDS in Africa are between the ages of 15 and 49 - in the prime of their working lives, AIDS weakens economic activity by squeezing productivity, adding costs diverting productive resources, and depleting skills. Thus, it has a negative effect on the process of development the African countries are attempting to achieve. With regard to the health sector, HIV/AIDS is bringing additional pressure on the health sector of the affected countries, particularly to sub-Saharan Africans. In these countries including Ethiopia about half of the hospital beds are occupied by HIV patients. This has a negative effect on the non-HIV patients since it creates problems reducing their chances of recovery when they are forced to be admitted only at later stages of illness.

Education is a key to social, cultural, and political participation, personal and community economic empowerment, and national development. Its output is the human capital which constitutes the nations primary wealth and potential for growth (Badcock-Walters, 2008). HIV/AIDS has been a major threat for this process. The epidemic not only affects the workforce in the sector but it also increases the number of dropouts of children as a result of parent's death. Particularly girls are vulnerable to dropout to compensate for loss of income through parent's sickness and related expenses, to care for sick relatives and to perform domestic work.

HIV/AIDS is affecting women and girls in increasing numbers. In sub-Saharan Africa 57 percent of adults with HIV are women and girls while in the world they accounted for 50 percent in 2003. Women are 1.3 times more likely to be infected with HIV than their male counterparts. Especially young women aged 15-24 years are three to six times more likely to be infected than young men (UNAIDS, 2004). There are many factors contributing for women's vulnerability among others some are social and economic inequality, biological factors, cultural inequalities, violence and so on.

There were orphans in the past, are at present and will be in the future because there will always be children who have had the misfortune to lose parents in one way or another. However, children who lost one or both parents of HIV/AIDS are not the same as those who lost their parents by other cases. Not only does HIV/AIDS affected families mean children lose their parents or guardians, but sometimes it means they lose their childhood as well because of the trauma and hardship that children affected by HIV/AIDS are forced to bear. As parents and family members become ill, children take on more responsibility to earn an income, produce food and care for family members. It is harder for these children to access adequate nutrition, basic health care, housing and clothing (USAID, 2010)

These children do not only suffer during their parent's illness but in the long run they will be orphaned. In African countries AIDS is generating orphans so quickly to the extent that family structures can no longer cope. Traditional safety nets are changing as more young adults are died of AIDS related illnesses (UNICEF, 2009).

The already poor families and communities need support for themselves, let alone take care of the orphans. Therefore, these orphaned children are forced to live either with foster parents, grandparents, and other relatives or live alone in child-headed households. The effect of HIV/AIDS on households is severe. Morbidity and mortality of individual effects on various institutions to which they belong. The household is one of these institutions and is severely affected by the epidemic. The declining productivity of HIV-positive individuals is initially felt within the family. It is pointed out in AVERT.ORG (2004) that as a result of death of productive household members, there will be loss of income and productive capacity, as well as increased costs and changing expenditure patterns.

Thus its effect will not end at the individual level. It further affects the household because most of the time in developing countries, it is the bread winner who is primarily affected by AIDS. Therefore, the survivors will be forced to face not only the problem of loss of one of the family member but also lack of resources such as income for livelihood. (Barnett, Whiteside and Desmond, 2000) had defined effect as: a shock to an existing system of livelihood at the national, regional, communal, or household level, which reduces the levels and expectations of life and welfare. It may mean the dissolution of the unit and the loss of individuals from poverty related causes rather than as a direct result of HIV/AIDS illness or death. Therefore, this research is guided by the above definition as HIV/AIDS affects households by reducing their living standard in combination with the existing poverty.

The effect of HIV/AIDS is not the same in all countries, communities or households. It depends on the level of development and coping mechanisms. Primarily, poor countries are vulnerable in general and poor households in particular because of many reasons. These countries are so poor to the extent that many people do not have access to the mass media; HIV/AIDS has been widespread making its prevention and control difficult. Poverty aggravates its spread because many people in poor developing countries primarily care about what to eat first rather than how to prevent HIV/ADS and only about one in five people at risk of HIV have access to prevention information and services (UNFPA, 2009).

In Africa, Fewer than five percent of the people in need get anti-retroviral drugs and prevention efforts have failed, large numbers of people are infected, would fail ill, and die (Barnett and Whiteside, 2002). These people are not only in need of care and support but they also leave behind families and orphans, many of whom will be impoverished. It is true that well resourced communities and households will be better able to cope than poor ones Bidpa (2000). Fenton (2004) noted that, as awareness of the epidemic has grown wealthier populations have been more able to access prevention messages and the means of prevention and the pattern of infection might be shifting towards those with lower socioeconomic status.

HIV/AIDS increases poverty at all levels from individual to nation through its effect on working age population. At the global level there is a positive correlation between HIV prevalence and poverty Fenton (2004). Many other factors also contribute to poverty; among others: poor health, illiteracy, social exclusion, and gender discrimination are the major ones. The effect of HIV/AIDS starts when an individual is infected and start to fall ill, which creates additional expense for health care, incapacitate the individual from working, and finally causes the death of the person. The morbidity and mortality among this working age group affects household incomes (UNAIDS, 2010).

2.6 The Effect of HIV/AIDS in Africa

HIV/AIDS is becoming an obstacle for development efforts in African countries. It is deepening poverty, reversing human development achievement, worsening gender inequalities, hindering government efforts to give essential services and reducing the labor force (UNDP, 2001). HIV/AIDS is aggravating the already existing poverty in developing African countries. Moreover, it has been at the top of their agenda because it is a big challenge to achieve their millennium development goals (ECA, 2003).

Among the eight-millennium declaration goals the first is to eradicate extreme poverty and hunger World Bank (2004), while HIV/AIDS is depleting assets of countries by increasing consumption and health care expenses. And the other goal is to improve child health, while in most African countries let alone improving, child health is worsening because of loss of income of parents affected by HIV/AIDS in particular and health sector of the country in general.

According to UNAIDS (2003), a lot of money has been disbursed and commitments made for AIDS programs in developing countries. In 2003 the project spending by different international institutions and organizations was estimated to be US$ 2.6 billion, as compared to US$ 1.2 billion in 2001. The same source reveals that in May 2003, US President George W. Bush signed legislation authorizing an increase in US government spending on HIV/AIDS, from US$ 5 billion to US$ 15 billion over the last five years. For example as of end of 2003, Ethiopia has got from the World Bank and Global Fund commitments of US$ 59.7 million and US$ 55.4 million respectively. From these figures we can see that the response to HIV/AIDS has forced these poor African countries as well as the donor agencies to divert their resources to fight HIV/AIDS.

If this much resources were spent on development programs the millennium development goals would have been reached to some extent. Therefore, it is certain that HIV/AIDS has a negative effect on poverty reduction strategies in developing countries. And also has been an obstacle to achieve the millennium development goals (UNAIDS, 2011).

The effects of HIV/AIDS in Africa are multifaceted. These include its effect on demography, the health sector, education sector, households, work place, etc. Effects of HIV at household level reflect all the above mentioned effects and this study focuses on the effect of HIV/AIDS on households, specifically in the study area. Effects of HIV at household level are reflected in the following way: one can see the demographic effect when both parents die leaving children behind; the size of the members in the family will be reduced; and also when affected family members are ill, the cost for health care increased (Richter, 2004).

In response to the epidemic, three main coping strategies appear to be adopted among affected households. First, savings are used up or assets sold; secondly, assistance is received from other households; and thirdly, the composition of households tends to change, with fewer adults of prime working age in the households. In addition to these coping mechanisms, affected households and individuals are seeking/receiving support from different NGOs, government organizations, and also from different social networks such as the extended families (UNFPA, 2010).

In most cases the burden of coping rests on women, as there is an increased demand for their labor for household work, childcare and care of the sick. As men fall ill, women often have to step into their roles outside the homes. In parts of Zimbabwe, for example, women are moving into the traditionally male-dominated carpentry-industry. This often results in women having less time to prepare food and for other tasks at home (AVERT.ORG, 2004).

2.7 Effects of HIV/AIDS in Ethiopia

In Ethiopia HIV/AIDS infections were first identified in 1984, and the first AIDS cases were reported in 1986 (Garbus 2003, Kloos and Hailemariam, 2004). The major mode of HIV transmission in the country is heterosexual which accounts for 87 percent of infections. Another 10 percent occur due to mother to child transmission and the remaining 3% is through blood contact.

Since then the numbers of infections have been increasing to the extent that almost everybody is affected directly or indirectly by the epidemic. According to IRIN (2004), HIV/AIDS patients occupy almost half the 12000 hospital beds in Ethiopia. By 1989, HIV prevalence among the general adult population was estimated to be 2.7 percent, 7.1 percent in 1997 and increased to 7.3 percent in 2000, and was 4.4 percent in 2004 of which 12.6 percent is urban and 2.6 percent rural. The decrease of the prevalence rate in 2004 may not reveal that HIV/AIDS infection has been reduced in the country. It further decreased to 2.3 percent in 2009 and 1.5 percent (DHS, 2011).

There are many factors which contribute to the low reported incidences, among others some could be the following. Prevalence rates are very low in rural communities; people are already infected with HIV but are not yet showing any of the symptoms of AIDS-related illnesses; people are already sick with AIDS-related illnesses but their illness is misdiagnosed; people are already sick and dying from AIDS but the community is in a state of denial and maintaining a state of secrecy. It is estimation about 7 to 10 million Ethiopians will be infected because of the high rate of adult prevalence, widespread poverty, low educational levels, and the government's limited capacity to respond (Garbus, 2003).

HIV/AIDS also highly affects the life expectancy of the country that shows loss of many people due to the epidemic. Recently it shows a slow trend of recovery because of lifelong drug and other care and support works which increases quality of life of AIDS patients and their families.

Ethiopia is one of the poorest countries in the world where about 80 percent of its population live in rural areas. This population is not only living in rural areas but also are illiterate and lack access to mass media, even to the radio. Poverty combined with illiteracy and inaccessibility to information has aggravated the spread of HIV/AIDS in the country. People are concerned more with the basic necessities such as food rather than HIV/AIDS, which is said to have an effect after a long time (Alemtsehay and Tsegazeab, 2008).

As a result, many people from rural areas are migrating to urban areas like Bahir Dar with the imagination that the city is more convenient for a living. However, when they arrive in the city, they find a different situation. Since they do not have anywhere to shelter, women are forced to work as a housemaids. Then most of them find it difficult to continue this work because it becomes beyond their expectation. Thus, mostly they start to work in Bars, which exposes them to be sex workers, and finally get infected with HIV/AIDS.

After they became infected and fall ill, they do not want to go back to their parents in rural areas because of the stigma and humiliation. They prefer to search support from NGOs or other organizations. Those with the better social networks will be lucky to get the support, while the other will go out the street (CARE International, 2010).

Ethiopian women are not only infected and affected when they migrate from rural areas. They are also more vulnerable when a specific household is affected by HIV/AIDS. They are responsible to care for the ill member of the family, where most of the time, the first to be sick is the breadwinner. At this time they do not only lose their husband, but they will be responsible to take care of themselves and the rest of the family members, of course, if they are not also sick because most probably they are infected with HIV. After the death of both or one of their parents, children will be orphans and girls are more likely to drop out of school to care for the ill, for domestic activities and/or engage in income generating activities such as sex work (FHAPCO & MWCY OVC Guideline, 2010).

The effect of HIV/AIDS at the household level increases the number of orphans. A UNAIDS report (2002) estimates that there were 990,000 AIDS orphans in Ethiopia at the end of 2001, and the MOH projected that the number of orphans would rise to 2.5 million in 2010 and it increases to more than 5 million by 2012. It is true that the increasing number of orphans will burden elders or grandparents, extended families and the community. Particularly the extended family is directly affected by the epidemic because usually they are the one who will take care of the orphans after the death of parents (Pankhurst, 2004). There are few governmental institutions for orphans in Ethiopia, as extended families usually take the victims in. These families themselves are likely to be poor and have to share their resources with the orphaned relatives as well as to their own families. Thus they are being impoverished (Garbus, 2003).

2.8 Effects of HIV/AIDS in Bahir Dar City

Even though Bahir Dar, Amhara regional City is benefiting from its natural location and being political center of the region that creates greater opportunities for its fast growth, most people of the City are facing many socioeconomic problems. The main problems are rural-urban migration, Alcohol, drug, chat and HIV/AIDs which are inter related one to the other. Many youth migrate from the surrounding rural woredas to the

City hopping better employment opportunities. These migrants are illiterate and cannot afford the cost of life in the City which causes them to engage in prostitution and day laborer works that aggravates the prevalence rate of HIV transmition which is 1.6% above the national of 1.5% (Amhara regional HAPCO, 2012).

As a result, about 14,000 People living with HIV (Felegehiwot Referral Hospital, 2013) and 9,033 orphan vulnerable children (Mekidum Bahir dar child survey index, 2012) in the City are still remaining needy due to the effects of HIV/AIDS despite the efforts of the government, NGOs, CBOs to mitigate the effects of HIV/AIDS. The absence of family tie due to migrants from the surrounding rural woredas especially complicates the care and support services to the poor PLHIVs and orphan vulnerable children (Bahir Dar City HAPCO, 2012).

Although the effects of HIV/AIDS are revealed in the day to day life of individuals and households, as well as on different sectors, there is no report based on studies about the effects of the epidemic on Bahir Dar City households and extended family system, particularly in affected household's livelihood areas. Since HIV/AIDS affects most economically active members of the household, it results in decline in income, savings and increasing expenditure for health care and funeral related costs

(DOH, 2013). This study focuses on; the effect of HIV/AIDS on household level livelihood and food security in Bahir Dar City, can serve for better further study and appropriate design of interventions.

2.9 The Effect of HIV/AIDS on Gender

The actual life of women and men reveals that there is variation in personal, physical, social and economic power and capacities between them. This results in differential rates of risk, infection patterns, access to health knowledge and protection, intervention and management of illness (Commonwealth Secretariat, 2002). There is a changing pattern in rates of male/female HIV/AIDS infections. According to UNAIDS (2004), in sub-Saharan Africa women are 30% more likely to be HIV-positive than men; 15-24 old African women, on average are 3.4 times more likely to be infected than their male counterparts.

Specifically, in informal and shanty settlements of most cities in developing countries, up to 50 per cent of households are headed by women, who typically rank among the poorer segments of the population; and most of them are migrants from the countryside. Once there, they live and work under the constant threat of eviction, crime, violence, HIV/AIDS and the daily dangers of unhygienic public toilets. Current statistics show that between 58 and 60 per cent of people infected with HIV/AIDS in sub-Saharan Africa are women. Research conducted by the African Population and Health Research Centre showed that women in informal settlements are more vulnerable to HIV/AIDS infection than their non-informal counterparts. This is largely the result of the extreme deprivation that prevails in informal settlements. High levels of unemployment, unstable sources of income and the predominance of low-paying jobs push many women into prostitution to supplement household incomes (UNAIDS, 2007).

The effect of AIDS on women is multifaceted. The existing inequality among men and women in combination with poverty and HIV/AIDS makes the lives of women worse than ever. In many countries including Ethiopia women are more vulnerable than men because of many factors among others the main ones being biological, cultural, social and economic. Women are caregivers, producers, guardians of family life, face greater economic insecurity because women are more likely to be poor than men (Commonwealth Secretariat, 2002). In addition, they have less entitlement to assets and savings, less secure employment, are uneducated, lack information, have little power in sexual negotiation, and so on.

The societal expectation that women will be the prime or only caregivers for their infected family members creates disproportionate social and economic burdens on them. According to Steinberg et al., (2002) in a study conducted in South Africa, in more than two thirds of households women or girls were the primary caregivers. A quarter of caregivers (23%) were over the age of 60 and just less than three quarters of these were women.

In Ethiopia a study revealed that 50.9 percent of women believed that a husband is justified in beating his wife if she refuses sexual relations (Garbus, 2003). Because of their economic dependency, many women fear that they will be abandoned by their husbands or supporting partners if they try to exert control over how and when they have sex and whether their partner uses a condom.

In addition, women are also disadvantaged in having access to education that affects their personal income and lower their status, which creates greater vulnerability to HIV infections. In case of death of parents or loss of income due to illness, girls are more likely to be withdrawn from school to perform household work and care for sick family member. And especially female headed households tend to become poorer than households headed by men (Richter, 2004).

In Ethiopia, girls who lost one or both parents are mostly forced to take care of the household and other siblings. In case of shortage of income, they are involved in income generating activities such as being housemaid and in risky works like prostitution. Sometimes, they are also vulnerable to be raped by a member of the extended family who was supposed to be responsible to take care of the orphans. Finally, girls like their parents are also exposed to HIV infection.

This particular study, with regard to gender, looks at how households have been affected by HIV/AIDS and become impoverished, how women are exposed to different problems such as economic, social, and cultural when their husbands die, how many households became female headed, how grandmothers are mostly responsible to take care of the orphaned grandchildren.

And also why women are more vulnerable to HIV/AIDS than men is because of economic dependency.

2.10 Socioeconomic Effect of HIV/AIDS on households

The socioeconomic effect of HIV/AIDS on households is multidimensional. As soon as one of the household members is affected by HIV/AIDS, the problem starts from psychological strain being afraid of the existing stigma. In addition to this income of the household will reduce because of lack of employment or increasing cost for health care. Since income is reduced, the expenditure for basic necessities will be reduced as well. According to a study made in South Africa affected households allocated more of their resources to food, health care and rent, and less to education, clothing, personal items and durables (Booysen, et al, 2001). Thus, unless there is another means of income and support outside the family, the affected household will be entering in deeper poverty in addition to the existing one. Apart from lack of income and basic necessities, after the death of the ill person, mostly the breadwinner, children will be orphaned.

In the household, women are the most vulnerable because of many reasons among them some are: they are responsible to care for the sick, for doing domestic work, and also to engage in income generating activities such as sex work and being housemaids. Therefore, the effect of HIV/AIDS and the coping mechanism of the households depend on different circumstances. According to Barnett and Whiteside (2002) and Baylies (2002), the effects of illness and death in households depend on the following. The number of cases the household experiences; the characteristics of the deceased individual such as age, gender, income and cause of death; the households composition and asset array, the attitude of the community to help the needy households, and also the availability of resources from the community, government and NGOs.

From the above explanations we can identify the following two major issues to be considered in the study of social effect of HIV/AIDS.

a) Characteristics of the Household

A household is an institution, which is the basis for any community. It consists of parents and children and/or relatives living under the same roof, sharing resources. Barnett and Whitside (2000) have defined the household as "Any unit of habitual residence where some consumption and/or production may be undertaken in common and where some members may recognize culturally defined relationships of kinship and/or affinity where the members are related in some way". If we look at this definition carefully, when a specific household is affected by HIV/AIDS almost all members of the family are also affected in some way or another. However, some are specifically vulnerable to its effect. Primarily affected ones are one of the survivors of the partner especially the woman, orphans and the elderly. Secondly affected households are of the extended families.

Before the death of the breadwinner children are exposed to many problems. Because the income of the household declining either by loss of employment or by increasing cost of health care, the quantity and quality of food in the household can decrease. Thus there can be decline in nutritional status of the children as well. In addition to this, there may be school dropouts particularly for girls. Then after the death of one or both parents, children will be orphaned. These orphaned children will be forced to either join extended families, if they are well off, or to engage in income-generating activities. Girls may engage in high-risk activities such as sex work, and boys in criminal activities. Finally the increasing number of orphans affects the coping mechanisms in households and extended families in particular and in the community and the country in general.

b) Resource availability from the Community, the government and NGOs

The main actors in the development process are the State, NGOs, and the private sectors. These organizations should also be partners to combat HIV/AIDS since the epidemic is the main challenge for poverty reduction programs. The epidemic affects them directly by reducing their labor force. Thus the coping mechanisms of HIV/AIDS affected households depend on the availability of resources in these organizations. It depends whether the community, the government and the NGOs have available resources to help the affected families. AIDS affected households primarily depend on relatives or community support systems to cope with the crisis. Community support networks such as savings clubs; 'eddir' and 'eqqub' (rotating credit associations), Self Support Group (SSG) in case of Ethiopia, labor exchanging schemes, etc. are important networks of the community during hardship such as HIV/AIDS hazards.

"Rich communities may cope; poor ones may not be at all lacking the resources to organize effectively" (Barnett and Whiteside, 2002). Poor people or households are not capable to access these networks because of the already existing poverty. Wealthier households have better access to those networks. Therefore, the poor households in addition to their poverty, affected by HIV/AIDS are vulnerable to be more impoverished than before. In poor developing countries like Ethiopia, even if there are social networks, it is difficult to the community to help the HIV/AIDS affected households because of their limited resources. It is not only the affected households that are impoverished, particularly in Ethiopia the social networks such as 'Iddir' are being depleted of their assets because of payments for funerals and other related expenditures (FHAPCO, 2008).

2.11 Conceptual Framework

As we can see in the following framework, the effect of HIV/AIDS in affected households is multifaceted. Morbidity and mortality have exacted a more severe burden on affected households. Women are more vulnerable than men because of lack of access to resources and services such as education, employment, credit, information; they have little power to negotiate sex which exposes them to the epidemic and other sexually transmitted diseases. In addition, after illness/death of one of the household member women are responsible to care for the patient, for domestic chores. As a result of this girls may drop out of school and also may engage in income generating activities such as sex work.

Economically, HIV/AIDS has a dual effect: the expenditure and income effects of the household. With regard to the expenditure, firstly there is an increased cost of medical treatment for HIV positive members who are beginning to develop symptoms of AIDS, and are experiencing more frequent illnesses. However all households are not affected similarly. The well off have access to go to the better hospitals like the private ones while the poor go to the public ones. Secondly, there is additional cost for funeral when a person with AIDS dies. The costs related with death of a family member are very high particularly in Ethiopia because the cost is not only for funerals but also for feeding guests for a long period of time.

The additional expenditure for medical treatment and funerals combined with the already existing poverty in the HIV/AIDS affected households is aggravated. Therefore, HIV/AIDS affected households are more likely to be impoverished.

The other economic effect of the HIV/AIDS affected household is the income effect. The affected household will lose the income of the member died of AIDS. As a result of this, the surviving family members such as one of the partners, usually women, children and other dependents will be affected. Children especially girls will be forced to drop out of school; their nutritional status will decrease. In general because of shortage of income, they will face lack of access to health services, education, housing and the like. Thus, the living standard of the HIV/AIDS affected household will decline.

There are different strategies which affected households use to cope with HIV/AIDS. The major ones are withdrawing savings, selling household assets and searching assistance from NGOs, government and the extended family.

The effect of HIV/AIDS on households does not end with economic effects. The surviving family and the extended family will also be affected socially and psychologically. Firstly, they are affected psychologically because of stigma. Secondly, as soon as parents die, children will be orphaned which results in a burden for the extended family primarily and the community and the country as a whole. When children are not able to live alone because of the household's conditions, they will leave the house to join the extended family or if they do not have access to it, to an institution. However, in the Ethiopian case since there are no enough of such institutions, many of these kinds of orphans will be forced to become street children and prostitutes.

Furthermore, HIV/AIDS changes the household structure and the family size after a specific household is affected. After the death of the mature age/breadwinner, different types of households originate such as female headed, child headed, grandparent headed and dissolved households. As a result the extended families will be burdened because they usually take in the orphans and other relatives who need support. This makes the extended families livelihoods decline as they share their resources with the new family members joining them, which in turn increases the number of poor and food insecure households.

In most cases women are the surviving parent in the household. The problem is not only becoming heads of the household, but they also lack income. This is because they are dependent on their husbands primarily. When these surviving parents die, the family structure changes to be child headed, if they are grown-ups and capable of managing the house. However, if they are not capable to be self-reliant, extended families have to take care of them particularly the grandparents. As grandparents and close relatives take in the orphans, they share their resources as a result of which their living standard will decline. Then the number of poor households will be increased. When families in affected households lack the access to be supported by extended families, they will be dissolved. This means that children and other family members will be dispersed in different households in order to survive.

Conceptual Framework for the study of

Effect of HIV/AIDS on Urban livelihood

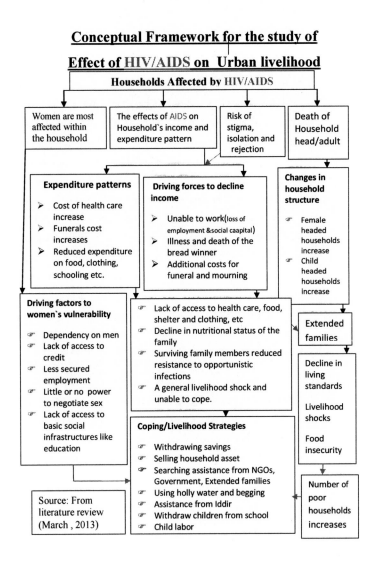

Chapter 3: RESEARCH METHODOLOGY

3.1 Description of the study area

Bahir Dar is the capital city of Amhara National Regional State which is situated in the north western part of the country. The City is located at a distance of 565 km away from Addis Ababa via Debremarkos to the North West direction. The altitude of the City is about 1800m above sea level and its climate is moderately hot. The monasteries found in the islands of Lake Tana to the north and `Tissisat` or Abay Falls which is 30 km away from the City to the south are the most tourist attractions of Bahir Dar. The Blue Nile River, its local name is Abay crosses four of seventeen kebele administrations of the City and flows to the south direction. The City has two administrative woredas and 17 kebeles (currently merged in to nine kebeles) with a total population of about 320,344 people (Bahir Dar Mayor Office, 2012).

The City has one main post office at the center and satellite offices in each kebele, digital micro wave and mobile telephone service. There is an international Air Port which is 10 km far to the west from the center which serves as a transit for tourists and local passengers to **Lalibela, Gondar and Axum**. There is also a main road which crosses the City and connects the center of the country to Tigray region and Sudan via Gondar.

Regarding health and education service; Bahir Dar City has one referral hospital, three health centers and owned by government and more than fifteen private clinics, and laboratories. There is one government owned University and more than 6 private colleges, three preparatory schools, three senior secondary school, ten junior and elementary schools, and more than eight kindergartens in the City.

Even though the City is benefiting from its natural location and being political center of the region that creates greater opportunities for its fast growth, most people of the City are facing many socioeconomic problems. The main problems are rural-urban migration and HIV/AIDs which are inter related one to the other. Many youth migrate from the surrounding rural woredas to the City hopping better employment opportunities. These migrants are illiterate and cannot afford the cost of life in the City which causes them to engage in prostitution and day laborer works (Bahir Dar City HAPCO, 2012).

As a result, many PLHIVs and OVC in the City are still remaining needy despite the efforts of the government, NGOs, CBOs to mitigate the effects of HIV/AIDS. The absence of family tie due to migrants from the surrounding rural woredas complicates the care and support services to the poor PLHIVs and orphan vulnerable children (Bahir Dar City HAPCO, 2012).

The study area was selected after assessing various organizations that support people living with HIV/AIDS (PLHIV) in different areas. This was done to meet the study objective, which aimed at examining the effect of HIV/AIDS on household livelihood and food security and also to assess its effect on the extended family. Since the subject of the study was mainly to be households and individuals affected by HIV/AIDS, an extensive assessment was made in order to find these subjects.

Firstly, Bahir Dar City Administration HIV/AIDS Prevention and Control Office (BHAPCO) was contacted in order to get the specific organizations from the members list of NGOs and GOs who are working on different activities particularly HIV/AIDS. According to the data found from BHAPCO, there are more than 8 local and 5 international NGOs involved in prevention and care of HIV/AIDS in Bahir Dar. Since it is difficult to communicate all these NGOs because of shortage of time and resource, some were selected purposively after contacting most of the NGOs inquiring about their involvement in HIV and AIDS.

It was found that some NGOs were working only on awareness giving activities and on orphans, while others were involved in supporting PLHIV. Two Associations namely Mekidum Ethiopia Bahir Dar Branch and Dawn of Hope Ethiopia Bahir Dar Branch are working on PLHIVs and Orphan almost with the same objectives and activities. These Associations are based on members of HIV positive people and Orphan vulnerable children form almost all kebeles of the city with strong referral linkages to avoid duplication.

Accordingly, Dawn of Hope Ethiopia Charity Association (DOH) that works for more than a decade in supporting HIV/AIDS patients and orphans and have relatively more clients in almost all kebeles of Bahir Dar city Administration was selected purposely to avoid complexity and ensure manageability. Therefore, the subjects for this study were selected from DOH's list of members (beneficiaries).

Dawn of Hope Ethiopia Bahir Dar branch (DOH) is a non for-profit non-governmental PLHIV association established in 2001 G.C by 3 males and 5 females founding members to fight against HIV/AIDS and to break the silence about the facts of the pandemic with slogan "Tiwlid Yidan Begna Yibka" equivalent meaning to `AIDS shall be stopped; let the generation be saved`. Since then, the association has done a lot on care and support, prevention, economic strengthening and legal protection issues for its members and the local community. It is the pioneer association that caused many associations in the region to being emerged and integrating for the response.

Currently, Dawn of Hope Ethiopia with its all 13 branches has registered in the new charity organization agency as local charity association. Dawn of Hope Bahir Dar as charity association, coordinated with its stakeholders and donors, is working strongly to contribute towards the achievement of the national goal of mitigating the effects and impacts of HIV/AIDS in the country. Its members are growing in number from 8 to more than 1171 of which 792 are females and 1006 members are on ART and 500 OVC of which 51 are HIV positive (DOH, 2012).

According to DOH program coordinator, the association is closely working with government sectors and non government organizations working in the City. The main activities are home based care, ART adherence, income generation activities(IGA), nutrition support for PLHAs and OVCs, school materials support for OVCs, rehabilitation service for chronic bed ridden clients, legal protection service coordinated with the concerned governmental sectors, community teaching and awareness rising, prevention works like condom distribution, testimonial service and positive living promotion.

3.2 Research Design

3.2.1 Analytic Framework

This study uses the Sustainable Livelihood Framework (SLF) to examine the effect of AIDS on the main components of the livelihoods in urban households. The Sustainable Livelihood Framework is an analytic tool developed by DFID. The Framework is based on the belief that 'people require a range of assets to achieve positive livelihood outcomes' (DFID, Sustainable Livelihoods Guidance Sheets 2008). The essential range of assets is grouped into the following five categories: Human Capital, Financial Capital, Physical Capital, Social Capital and Natural Capital.

The hypothesis is that AIDS is a shock that impacts all classes of assets and results in livelihood insecurity. Human capital is lost through chronic illness and death of prime age labor as well as loss of skills and knowledge transfer. Financial capital is undermined due to: i) increased health care & funerals expenditure, ii) reduced income (through loss of productivity),

iii) decrease in assets ownership (assets are sold to make up for lost income). Social capital is damaged as structures at the household and community level are affected. Physical and natural capitals are damaged through loss of labor which affects the ability to work and maintain common property.

In addition to the Sustainable Livelihood Framework, the study considered some food security proxy indicators. These are the Food Consumption Score which combines information on meal frequency and dietary diversity and the Coping Strategy Index which has proven to be a good indicator of food security level of the households (WFP, 2008).

3.2.2 Sample size determination

To calculate the sample size of HIV/AIDS affected and infected households, the following formula which is advisable for small population is used (Israel, Glen D. 1972)

$$n = \frac{N}{1 + N(e^2)}$$

Where; n = number of sample size
N = Total number of population
e^2 = level of precision

Using the above formula with 10% level of precision and 1,171 total number of population from DOH beneficiaries' list, 92

HIV infected household heads were selected as a base sample and by dividing base sample by the response rate (92/0.9) the final sample size is 102 HIV infected household heads.

3.2.3 Sampling Design

The study subjects were randomly selected from beneficiaries lists of an NGO (DOH) working with the community of Bahir Dar city. Two key informants from the government agencies (Head of the HIV/AIDS Prevention and Control Office, coordinator of the charity organization), and five home based caregivers from the community were selected purposively. From DOH`s beneficiaries list, 102 HIV/AIDS infected household heads were selected using systematic random sampling technique.

3.3 Data Collection and Instruments

3.3.1 Instruments

The study employed triangulation method, to support and check up the reliability of data obtained. The methods used to collect the data include in-depth interview using structured and semi-structured questionnaire, key informant interviews, focus groups discussions, and observation methods. All categories of data collection were conducted in Amharic after translating the questions from English to Amharic. Then again the Amharic version responses were translated into English for analysis.

3.3.2 Data Types and Collection Procedures

Primary data were collected for this study from household heads, government agencies, charity organization coordinator, and caregivers using structured questionnaire, semi-structured questionnaire, focus group discussions, and direct observation. The data focuses on human capital (mortality, skill and education level), financial capital (expenditure on food, expenditure on non food and total expenditure), physical capital (household equipments, housing condition and household saving), social capital (membership of Iddir, Equib and leadership role of the household in the community) and for food security (frequency of food intake per day among household members and Varity of food taken among household members within a week) were collected using structured questionnaire for both HIV infected and referred by health institutions for support to DOH. Additional data were obtained from focus group discussion among five home based care givers and some five randomly selected HIV affected household heads and key informant interviews.

3.4 Data Analysis

Microsoft excel was used for data entry. Then, the data was exported to STATA format for cleaning and analysis. The analysis was mainly done at household level. The household is the locus of three important decisions: demographic, production and consumption. Its character of being a unit of decision concerning individual members' activities and their consumption (and hence their welfare) makes it a useful sample unit with an identifiable location in survey work (World Bank, 1990:38). In view of these advantages, the analysis in this paper is mainly done at the household level.

The household survey data was used to estimate the statistical relationship between various food and livelihood security indicators. Both bi-variant and multivariate analyses were employed. In the bi-variety analysis, **cross tabulations and chi-square test** were applied to examine the association between each of the independent variables and the dependent variables. The chi-square test in the bi-variety analysis does not consider confounding effects. Therefore, for multivariate analysis, **multiple regression and logistic regression** is used. The parameter estimates of the models helps to analyze the net effects of each of the independent variables on the various dependent variables. The basic models in estimating the effects of various predictor variables on various dependent variables are presented below.

The Models for each specific objective are as follows;

▸ **Examine how HIV/AIDS affects the human capital of urban HIV infected and affected households.**

Dependent variable; human capital using a proxy variable of Income[1] (Y)

Independent variables; mortality, labor supply and education, consumption

Multiple Linear Regression Model; $Y_i = \beta + \beta_1 x_1 + \beta_{i2} x_2 + \beta_{i3} x_3 + \beta_{i4} x_{i4} + \epsilon_i$

Where; x_1 is mortality among household members during the last 12 months

x_{i2} is the labor supply (hour's household heads spend on work per day)

x_{i3} is the education level of the household heads

X_{i4} Consumption expenditures of households for 3 months

β Is the constant term, β_i are the parameters and ϵ_i is the error term.

---

[1] The assumption is that Human capital of a household is best explained by its sustainable income which is the result of education, health and able to work of the household members.

► **Probe into the effect of HIV/AIDS on the physical capital of urban HIV affected households.**

Dependent variable; Physical capital using a proxy variable of Asset[2] (HA)

Independent variables; Household illness, Household saving and household expenditure

Multiple Linear Regression Model; $HA = \beta + \beta_1 \times_1 + \beta_{i_2} \times i_2 + \beta_{i_3} \times i_3 + \epsilon i$

Where; $\times_1$ is the household illness

$\times i_2$ is the household saving

$\times i_3$ is the household food and non food expenditure

β is the constant term, βi are the parameters and ϵi is the error terms.

► **Explore the linkages between HIV/AIDS and financial capital of urban HIV affected households.**

Dependent variable; financial capital using a proxy variable of Household consumption expenditure[3] (HCS)

Independent variables; Income, Illness and Family size

---

[2] The assumption is that chronic illness of a household head or/and member causes degradation of household's physical capital such as sale of household articles and productive asset like land, house etc

[3] The assumption is that household's financial capital is best explained by household consumption expenditure because as illness and family size

Multiple Linear Regression Model; $HCS_i = \beta + \beta i_1 x_1 + \beta i2 \times i2 + \beta i3 \times i3 + \epsilon i$

Where; x_1 is household head illness at least for 3 months during the last 12 months

$\quad\quad x\, i_2$ is income of the household for 3 months

$\quad\quad x\, i_3$ is household family size

$\quad\quad \beta$ is the constant term, βi are the parameters and ϵi is the error terms.

▸ **Scrutinize food security status of households affected by HIV/AIDS.**

Food consumption score (FCS) developed by World Food Program (WFP) as a best household food security indicator that shows the "frequency of food intake per day among household members times the Varity of food the household members intake within seven days (a week) data" will be utilized to investigate the Adult Level food Consumption (ALC) of households' food security level as severely insecure <14, Temporarily insecure 14 – 21, moderately insecure 21 – 35 and food secure >35 ALC. "For example, if the household members eat 2 times per day two types of food for consecutive 7 days

increases households consumption expenditure increases and put pressure on income and savings of the households.

containing balanced diet i.e. 2x2x7=28 ALC whose score shows moderately food insecure".

Logistic Regression Model:

To control confounding effects and identify specific variables that affect the application of coping strategies, logistic regression model is utilized. Logistic regression model is an appropriate tool because the response or dependent variable is dichotomous (1 or 0, suggesting that the house hold has applied the specific coping strategy in the previous 30 days before the survey and did not apply, respectively). The predictor variables entered into the model may be categorical, quantitative, or a combination of the two. Suppose, the probability of applying the specific negative coping strategies Y, [P (Y=1)] depends on a set of explanatory variables X1, X2, X3, ..., Xk. The basic form of the logistic function is:

$$P = p \left(y = \frac{1}{x1,x2,x3,...xk} \right) = \frac{e^2}{1+e^2} = \frac{\exp(Z)}{1+\exp(Z)}$$

Where z, is a linear function of a set of predictor variables, X1, X2, X3, ... Xk , given by

Z = b0 + b1X1 + b2X2 + ... + bkXk, and b0, b1, b2 ... bk are regression coefficients.

Logit of P is derived by taking natural logarithm, that is, log $[(\frac{P}{P-1})] = Z$. The quantity $[(\frac{P}{P-1})]$ is called the odds and hence log $[(\frac{P}{P-1})]$, the log odds. These logit regression coefficients are used to compute odds ratios (OR), which are interpreted as the increased odds of a positive outcome on a dependent variable for the affirmative category (applied the specific coping strategy asked) (X=1) over "not applied" (X=0). The OR helps an estimate of the magnitude of association between the predictor variables and the dependent variable, application of the specific coping strategies.

CHAPTER 4: FINDINGS OF THE STUDY

The findings of the study are presented in five sections. In the first section, the effects of HIV/AIDS on human capital of the households are presented. The financial capital effects, physical capital effects and Social capital effects are discussed in the second, third and fourth sections of this chapter, respectively. Finally, the last section is devoted to the analysis of the effects HIV/ AIDS is causing on food security status of households.

Table 4.1 Socioeconomic and demographic description of households

Age	frequency	Percent
<=18 years old	2	2.0
19-25 years old	5	4.9
26-35 years old	49	48.0
36-45 years old	30	29.4
46-55 years old	10	9.8
56-65 years old	5	4.9
66-75 years old	1	1.0
Total	102	100.0

Source: Household Survey (2013)

The age of the majority respondents concentrates around (26 – 45) years which is the productive and reproductive age.

Household family size of the majority (32.4%) respondents is three, (20.6%) have four, and (17.6%) have two and one. The mean household size of the households' family size is 2.9.

As the table below shows household heads married (31.4%), widowed (36.3%), divorced (29.4%) and (2.9%) are separated. The majorities of respondents are either widowed or divorced.

Table 4.2 Marital Status of Respondents

Marital status	Frequency	Percent
Married	32	31.4
Widowed	37	36.3
Divorced	30	29.4
Single	3	2.9
Total	102	100.0

Educational level	Frequency	Percent
Illiterate	48	47.1
Grade (1 - 5)	10	9.8
Grade (6 - 8)	21	20.6
Grade (9 - 12)	19	18.6
College/higher	4	3.9
Total	102	100.0

Table 4.3 Educational level of respondents

Table 4.4 Household heads occupation

Occupation	Frequency	Percent
No occupation	5	4.9
Gov't employ	5	4.9
private sector	8	7.8
Petty Trade	39	38.2
Sex worker	1	1.0
Local liquor	2	2.0
Handcrafts	1	1.0
Agriculture	1	1.0
NGO employ	4	3.9
Homemade	4	3.9
Daily laborer	29	28.4
House wife	1	1.0
Others	2	2.0
Total	102	100.0

Source: Household Survey (2013).

The employment condition of the respondents as presented on the table shows that the greater number of respondents (38.2%) were working as petty trader (small retailing business) and the (28.4%) were working as day laborer.

4.2 HIV/AIDS and Human Capital

Human capital is comprised of the knowledge, skills and good health that enable people to work in order to pursue livelihood outcomes. Hence, household human capital is determined by the quantity and quality of labor availability which, in turn, depends upon several factors, such as household size, age structure, skill and knowledge levels as well as Mental, Psychological and physical health status. AIDS affects the quantity and quality of productive labor through the death and chronic illness of household members in productive and reproductive age group, through the amount of time taken by others to care for the chronically sick (taking into account HIV/AIDS is a protracted illness), time lost during customary mourning period and loss in knowledge/ skills transfers.

4.2.1 Mortality and Chronic Illness due to HIV/AIDS

In this study, out of the 102 households surveyed, 39 households (38.2%) reported they were sick at least for three months and 18 households (17.6%) reported their usual family member died during the last 12 months preceding the survey. According to the study results, 38.2 percent of the respondents were unable to work at least for 3 months that causes additional income reduction on the already impoverished households. This also shows us that they were not able to contribute labor to the labor market that further affects the healthy functioning of the economy. Death of a household member especially household head declines the labor supply of the household and hence income and increases funeral related cost.

The chi square test below shows that HIV/AIDS sickness and death of household members due the epidemic is significantly related.

Deceased family members in the last 12 months of HIV/AIDS affected/infected households, 9 (50%) are died of TB, 6 (33.3%) are died of Diarrhea while the remaining 3(16.7%) are died of Pneumonia and malaria. From this we can say that TB is the major co-factor/opportunistic disease that aggravates the illness and death of HIV/AIDS patients.

All the deceased family members are between the ages of 19 – 65 years old which is the productive and reproductive age that confirms AIDS is rely a bottleneck of development. As to the relationship of the deceased with in the household, it shows that out of 18 deaths 12 (66.6%) are household heads (HHH) and the remaining 33.4% are Spouses, Son/Daughter or other family members which also witnesses that the bread winner of the household are seriously affected by the diseases which exposes the family to remain needy and vulnerable.

Moreover, a high percentage of the deceased (66.6 %) were household heads. One implication is loss of knowledge/skills, including skills to manage socioeconomic activities. Another implication is that the remaining spouse is responsible for both economic activities and to head the household. Unfortunately with HIV AIDS the remaining spouse will also be sick.

4.2.2 Education and Economic Activities of HIV/AIDS Affected Households

Education attainment is one of the main indicators of human capital of the households and directly relates to the livelihood conditions of people especially those living in urban areas. Household heads were asked in order to check their level of education attainment based on the principle that; How do you think urban life with unable to even read and write? To understand the relationship between households educational attainment and their economic activity such as household saving, the cross tabulation analysis table 4.5 below shows 48(47.1%) of the respondents are illiterate (unable to read and write) and 26 (54%) households of them have no saving where as out of 54 literate (able to read and write) households, only 22 (40.7%) households have no saving and the remaining 32 households have savings in formal financial institutions. This shows that as household heads are able to read and write their economic activity like saving increases.

Table 4.5 Education level respondents attained and their savings

		Do you save Money?						
		No	ACSI	CBE	Other banks	Equib	saving box	Total
Education	No	26	13	3	2	2	2	48
	Yes	22	25	2	2	3	0	54
	Total	48	38	5	4	5	2	102

Source: Own Survey (2013)

The chi square test below shows that education and households saving (economic activity) are significantly related as the education level of respondents increases their savings in the formal financial institutions like ACSI (Amhara credit and saving institutions) and other banks.

Respondents were also asked about their knowledge of HIV virus transmition ways and more than 90% of them know ways of transmition such as unprotected sexual practices, sharing

87

sharpen tools and mother to child transmition during pregnancy, delivery and burst feeding. But out of 102 respondents 32(31.4%) reported that Mosquito insect can transmit HIV virus which shows that they lack knowledge that HIV can never be transmitted by insects.

4.2.3 HIV/AIDS and Economic Activities of Respondents

Respondents were asked if they were too sick for at least 3 months during 12 months preceding the survey. As shown from table 4.6 below, out of 102 household heads 36(35.3%) were sick and unable to work for three and more months and the remaining 66(64.7%) were not sick and able to work. These 35.3 percent of household heads who were unable to work and thus can't generate income for their households that exposes them either to sale household assets or remain food insecure.

Table 4.6 Unable to work because of illness at least for 3 months during past 12 months

	Frequency	Percent
No	66	64.7
Yes	36	35.3
Total	102	100.0

Source: Own Survey (2013)

According to the survey results indicated on table 4.7 below, household heads were asked about their main economic activity/occupation. Out of 102 respondents the majority 39(38.2%) were engaged on petty trading, the so called ('gulit') like informal retailing of onion, potato, charcoal, vegetables, etc. in the village and along sides of the road). Next to petty traders 29(28.4%) were day laborers mostly working in the construction sector and among others 8(7.8%) were working as waiters in the café and bars.

Table 4.7 Respondents major economic activity

Types of occupation	Frequency	Percent
No occupation	5	4.9
Government employ	5	4.9
private sector	8	7.8
Petty Trade	39	38.2
Commercial sex worker	1	1.0
Local liquor	2	2.0
Artisans/handcrafts	1	1.0
Agriculture	1	1.0
NGO employ	4	3.9
Non paid housemaids	4	3.9
daily laborer	29	28.4
House wife	1	1.0
Others	2	2.0
Total	102	100.0

Source: Household Survey (2013)

Estimated means of regression analysis of households' economic activity versus their educational attainment shows that as respondents' educational level increases from grade zero (illiterate) to grade 5, number of housemaids decreases gently and as education level further increases number of housemaids decreases sharply. Number of petty traders decrease sharply as their education level increases from illiterate to grade 5 and it increases sharply as their education level increases to grade 8 and further increases gently as they have got more and more educated. Number of daily laborers increase gently as their education level increases from illiteracy to grade 5 and increases sharply as their education level increases further to grade 8 but as we can observe from the chart below decreases sharply as household heads attend higher education beyond grade 8.

NGO employees (volunteers such as home based care givers, ART adherence promoters employed by NGOs) have attended grade 8 and above while Government sector employees have attended grade 12 and more. Number of Private sector employees (waitress in café, restaurants and bars) increases sharply as their education level increases from grade 5 to grade 8 and increases further gently as their educational level increases to grade 12 and decreases sharply as their educational level increases beyond grade 12.

char1. Economic activity Vs Education level of respondents

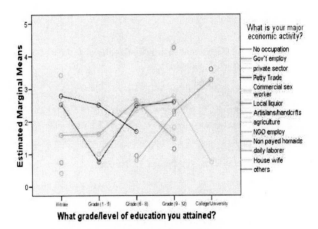

Non-estimable means are not plotted

Source: Own household Survey Estimated means (2013)

Therefore, from the above chart we can see that household heads educational attainment level determines their economic activities and hence incomes. Illiteracy is the main enemy of development endeavors and even complicated the care and support programs of the government and non-governmental organizations. An illiterate is engaged in jobs which may expose to HIV infection such as prostitution and once infected by the virus is too poor to take ART as prescribed and results in bed ridden or death than the literate once.

4.2.4 Regression Analysis Results of Human Capital of HIV affected Households

The regression of respondents income (Y) as main proxy indicator of human capital on households education (E), Consumption expenditures of households (Ex), Labor Supply/economic activity by hours spent on work (L) and mortality during the last 12 months (M) shows that households education and economic activity/labor supply positively affects household's income (human capital) while the mortality of respondents negatively affects their income as the model and analysis results presented below.

$Y = 2.484$	$+ 0.402Ex +$	$0.270E$	$+ 0.091L$	$-$	$0.170M$
se	0.415	0.091	0.087	0.099	0.098
t	(5.990)	(4.410)	(3.113)	(0.929)	(-0.571)
		$R^2 = 0.7693$			

92

The regression results above shows that a unit (grade) change in household head's educational attainment changes households' income by about 27%, working hours spent per day by household's member is not significant which indicates their income is not directly related to their working conditions while death of a household member decrease the household's income by about 17% that shows how HIV/AIDS affects human capital of households due to the death and inability to work for longer time. Households' consumption expenditure creates pressure on the household head and other active labor members of the family to work hard and able to generate better income. A household consumption is significant at 1% level and a unit change in consumption allocation changes the income of the household by about 40 percent which means 60 percent of their consumption expenditure is covered by support.

4.3 Financial Capital

Financial capital specifically refers to assets and entitlements that have a cash value. They include income; remittances from family members working away from home, sources of credit, pensions, savings and disability grant are important asset bases in the urban context.

4.3.1 Income of Households

Income is the magic spices that sweets livelihood's of mankind and is a main tool for decision making of a day to day life of human. But unfortunately, there is a wide gap of inequality of earning it. 102 household heads were asked how much income their households earned during the last 3 months.

The majority of the respondents 39(38.2%) reported that they have earned (2001 – 3000) Birr and 34(33.3%) of households have earned (1001 – 2000) Birr for three months. Table 4.9 below shows that most of the households were earning less than 1000 Birr per month and when it is divided by 2.9 (the average household family size of the respondents), each household member share about 345 Birr per month and this means 11.5 Birr per day which is about half a dollar that shows these households are below the poverty line of a dollar per day.

Table 4.9 Income households earned during the last 3 months

Household Income	Frequency	Percent
(200 - 1000)Birr	1	1.0
(1001 - 2000)Birr	34	33.3
(2001 - 3000)Birr	39	38.2
(3001 - 4000)Birr	12	11.8
(4001 - 5000)Birr	10	9.8
(5001 - 6000)Birr	6	5.9
Total	102	100.0

Source: Household Survey (2013)

4.3.2 Expenditure of Households

Household's expenditure on food and non food purchasing is one way to understand and measure livelihoods of the urban HIV affected people. The survey result shows below that out of 102 household heads 36(35.3%) were spending for food (2001 – 3000) Birr for three months preceding the survey, 29(28.4%) were spending for food (10001 – 2000) Birr and 22(21.6%) were spending for food (3001 - 4000) Birr while the remaining 15(14.7%) households were spending (4001 - 7001) Birr for food for three months. This also shows that households affected and infected by HIV have poor food consumption spending which degrades their quality of life and contributes a lot for the deterioration of their livelihood.

Table 4.10 Households spending for food for 3 months

Households` Spending	Frequency	Percent
(1001 - 2000)Birr	29	28.4
(2001 - 3000)Birr	36	35.3
(3001 - 4000)Birr	22	21.6
(4001 - 5000)Birr	8	7.8
(5001 - 6000)Birr	6	5.9
>=7001 Birr	1	1.0
Total	102	100.0

Source: Household Survey (2013)

Households were also asked to report their non – food consumption spending for three months preceding the survey. Out of 102 respondents 56(54.9%) household heads reported that their non food spending during the preceding three months was (1001 – 2000)Birr and 41(40.2%) household heads reported they were spending (200 – 1000) Birr while the remaining 5(4.9%) households were spending (2001 – 5000)Birr for non food for three months preceding the survey. During the survey respondents were listing house rent and fuel/charcoal expenses are the major challenges for their survival. The figures also shows that with urban life where everything is monetized and non food expenses are high, the HIV affected households are still remain with high food expenditure than non-food one which indicates that they are vulnerable and desperate.

Table 4.11 Households spending for Non-food for 3 months

Expenditure (Birr)	Frequency	Percent
(200 - 1000)	41	40.2
(1001 - 2000)	56	54.9
(2001 - 3000)	4	3.9
(4001 - 5000)	1	1.0
Total	102	100.0

Source: Household Survey (2013)

4.3.3 Household Saving and Loan

A household saving is a sign and status qua for the healthy functioning of day to day life of a household in particular and the whole economy in general. Saving is the difference between income and expenditure of households that shows the livelihood conditions of the household, as more and more they able to save their livelihood conditions are getting better and better. Out of 102 household heads interviewed 48(47.1%) household heads have no saving while 54(52.9%) have saving in different forms. The bar chart below shows that saving and education have a direct relationship as household heads are able to attend better grade of education their saving increases. Among the financial institutions ACSI (Amhara Saving and Credit Institution) takes the largest share (70.4%) followed by CBE (commercial Bank of Ethiopia) and Equib(voluntary informal revolving saving and credit group) each comprises (8.93%) and the remaining (11.7%)are shares of other private banks and within home savings

Figure 4.1 Households savings and financial institutions

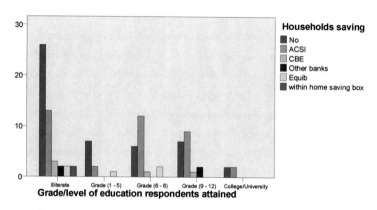

Source: Household Survey (2013)

Among 102 households asked about their loan condition during last 12 months, the majority 83(81.4%) did not get loan while only 19(18.6%) did get loan. As we can see from table 4.12 below out of 19 households 16(84.2%) had loan for the purpose of business development where as the remaining 3(15.8) households had loan for emergency health care, funeral and house furniture costs.

These shows that due to ART and better health care, HIV infected households are engaging in income generating activities and developing businesses. The majority of respondents are reluctant to take loan due to lack of knowledge, collateral and access of production and marketing places. Even to run small business which can be done at home, they need to have their own house because the owners of the houses do not allow renters to do so.

Table 4.12 purposes of households get money loan

Purposes	Frequency	Percent
No loan	83	81.4
Emergency health care	1	1.0
Business	16	15.7
Funeral related costs	1	1.0
House furniture	1	1.0
Total	102	100.0

Source: Household Survey (2013)

Regression Analysis of household financial spending on household's income, family size and illness of household head/member at least for 3 months during the last 12 months as table 4.13 below shows that households consumption spending have positive relation with family size and income while negative relation with illness of the household head.

The unit increase in households' income results an increase in households consumption spending by about 41.2%, an increase of a household member by one increases households consumption spending by about 2.9% and illness of a household head decreases households' spending by about 4.4% which means illness causes their income to decline further and results in a negative consumption from either asset disposal or supports by others as well as cut or reduce quality and quantity of food consumption. Illness due to HIV/AIDS is the major obstacle for the livelihoods' of urban infected and affected households. All the variables in the model are statistically significant that shows the strong relation between HIV sickness and consumption related expenses of affected households.

$$HFs = 1.979 + 0.412Y + 0.029Fs - 0.044IL$$

$$Se \quad 0.294 \quad\quad 0.087 \quad\quad 0.011 \quad\quad 0.021$$

$$t \quad (6.720) \quad (4.708) \quad (2.667) \quad (-2.036)$$

$$R^2 = 0.7639$$

Where:

HFs = Household's Financial monthly Spending

Y = Monthly Income of households

Fs = Family size of the respondents

IL = Illness of household head for 3 months during the last 12 months

Table 4.13 Regression analysis of household's expenditure on income, illness and family size

| Model | Unstandardized Coefficients | | Standardize Coefficient | | |
	B	Std. Error	Beta	t	Sig.
(Constant)	1.979	.294		6.720	.000
Sickness for 3 months	-.044	.021	-.119	-2.036	.045
Household Income	.412	.087	.424	4.708	.000
Household Family size	.029	.011	.115	2.667	.012

a. Dependent Variable: Households consumption spending

Source: Household survey (2013)

4.4 Physical Capital

This section focuses on effects of HIV/AIDS on Asset- related indicators of households.

4.4.1 Asset Ownership

Households were asked whether or not they own the various assets categorized as Jewelry, Electronics, and House furniture before and after they are being infected by HIV/AIDS Virus. As table 4.14 below shows out of 102 households 74(72.5%) of the household heads had assets and 28(27.5%) household heads reported they had no such assets before they are being infected and affected by the virus.

On the contrary, out of 102 household heads asked about their asset ownership after infected and affected by the virus 66(64.7%) households reported that they have no any asset and 36(35.3%) have these assets. This clearly shows that household heads who have these asked assets decreases from 74(72.5%) household heads before affected by the virus to 36(35.3%) after affected by the virus. On the other hand, household heads reported that they have no such assets increases from 28(27.5%) to 66(64.7%) which also means 38(37.3%) household heads sale their assets they had before because of the effects of HIV/AIDS for medication, funeral related costs and other household consumption.

Table 4.14 Assets such as Jewelry, Electronics, and House furniture before and after households affected by HIV

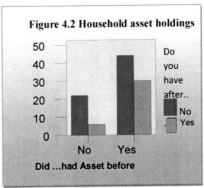

Figure 4.2 Household asset holdings

Source: Household Survey (2013)

The Chi Square test shows that Sickness and asset ownership of HIV/AIDS infected households have significant relationship. The cross tabulation result above shows that out of 39 household heads had been sick for at least 3 months during the last 12 months, 36 household heads have sold their household assets while 6 household heads did not sale assets. In addition, out of 63 households affected by the epidemic 33 households have no these asked assets while the remaining 30 households have these assets. This also shows that even though greater numbers of households with high sickness have sold their assets, others who are affected by the virus are still have sold their assets due to the pressure of the diseases on their ability to labor and earn income, lack of employment opportunity and opportunistic infection.

The regression result of households' asset holdings on the sickness of the household head/member, savings of the households and food support households have got during the last 6 months shows that sickness of a household head/member decreases the asset holdings of the household by about 31.9%, a unit change in the households' saving changes the household asset holdings by about 3% and having access for food support increases households asset holdings by about 11.3% which shows food support for affected households helps them to protect asset degradation and increase their savings as well as asset forma

$$HA = 0.390 + 0.030S + 0.113Fs - 0.319IL$$

Se 0.083 0.038 0.091 0.094

t (4.710) (0.779) (1.245) (-3.382)

$$R^2 = 0.9982$$

Where; HA = Households Physical Asset Holdings

S = Savings of households at any financial institutions

Fs = Food support households received during the last 3 months

IL = Illness at least for 3 months during the last 12 months

Shelter is a very important component of basic human life and can be considered as one indicator of people's livelihood condition especially in urban areas. Housing ownership condition among urban HIV/AIDS affected and infected households and quality of the house they are living in are presented in the form of cross tabulation below.

Out of 102 household heads asked about their household house ownership condition the majority of respondents 45(44.1%) are living in private rented house, 34(33.3%) of households have their own house, 18(17.6%) are living in kebele rented houses, 3(2.9%) are sharing with other people and the remaining 2 household heads are reported they are living in other conditions. In general 50(49%) of the respondents have no their own house and are in difficulty conditions as compared to those who have their own house and rented from kebele. Moreover, households reported about the materials made of their living houses that 91(89.2%) are living in a house its roof is made of tin, 9(8.8%) are living in houses its roof is made of plastic and the remaining 2(1.96%) are living in houses its roof is made of wood and straw. The wall of whose houses made of mud are 75(73.5%), whose house's wall are made of wood are 19(18.6%), whose house's wall are made of concrete are 3(2.94%) and 4(3.92%) are reported that their house's wall are made of tin while 1 household is living in a house its wall is made of plastic.

96(94.12%) households are living in houses its floor are mud and the remaining 6(5.88%) households are living in houses its floor are concrete.

Table 4.17 House ownership conditions of HIV affected households

Housing condition	Frequency	Percent
Rent from kebele	18	17.6
rent from private	45	44.1
Owen	34	33.3
Free hold	1	1.0
Others	1	1.0
Sharing	3	2.9
Total	102	100.0

Source: Household Survey (2013)

Figure 4.3 below shows that out of 102 households 71(69.6%) are living in a single class, 24(23.5%) households are living in a house comprises of two classes and 7 households are living in houses having 3 and 4 classes. From the above table and figure results, it is clear that the majority of households affected by HIV/AIDS are living in a poor quality of houses that further complicates their health conditions. Homelessness or not better than that is a condition which further deteriorates their livelihoods and brings social and psychological effects on these already impoverished HIV/AIDS affected households.

Figure 4.3 House ownership condition and number of classes

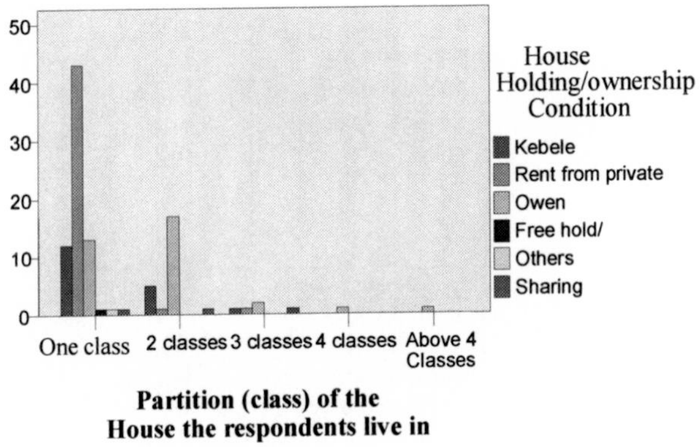

Partition (class) of the
House the respondents live in

Source; Household Survey (2013)

4.4.2 Water and Hygiene Conditions of Households

Access for potable water and better hygiene condition improves the health status of people infected and affected by HIV/AIDS. Households are asked about their access for pure water and toilet. Among 102 households interviewed, 93(91.2%) household heads reported that their household members are accessed to pure piped water the remaining 7 households get water from public bono and 2 households are getting from ground water.

Table 4.18 Respondents access to clean water and Latrine/Toilet

Water accesses	Frequency	Percent
private piped water	93	91.2
public Bono	7	6.9
Ground water	2	2.0
Total	102	100.0

Toilet accesses	Frequency	Percent
piped and sewage latrine/Toilet	3	2.9
traditional latrine/toilet	76	74.5
VIP(ventilated improved pits)	9	8.8
Open defecation on road sides	14	13.7
Total	102	100.0

Source: Household Survey (2013)

Out of 102 respondents about their household toile access, 76(74.5%) have access for traditional toilet and 14(13.7%) are using open pts (on road sides, on River and lake banks, bushes etc.), 9(8.8%) households have access for ventilated and improved pit and only 3(2.9%) households have access for piped and sewage toilet. Overall, 99 households out of 102 respondents have no access for sewage and piped toilet and poor hygienic that further bring health complication.

In general, the physical capital of most households as presented above all the asset ownership, access for house, water and hygiene conditions shows that HIV infected and affected households are poor, desperate and highly marginalized. They sold assets such as gold and other jewelries, electronics equipments and house furniture due to the illness and death of their families. The housing conditions also show that most of them are living in rented house which is poor in quality and have no access for better toilet that further complicates their hygiene and health conditions.

4.5 Social Capital of Households

Building social assets can increase the chances of greater self-reliance amongst households and neighborhoods. Social capital refers to the network of support and reciprocity that may exist within and between households and within communities, which people can call on in times of stress. Out of 102 household heads asked whether they are getting food and other social support from relatives and friends who are not living in their household during the last 12 months and 101(99%) of them reported that they have no such relatives and friends who can support them.

102 household heads were asked about their participation in community Iddir (social support group especially during stress like funeral and other social phenomena). Out of interviewed

household heads 57(55.9%) have Iddir while 45(44.1%) have no Iddir. Among those households who have no Iddir 24.5% households reported that they have no Iddir because of poverty, 10.7% are because they have no permanent residence, 5.9% of household heads have no reason and 2.9% household heads reported that they have no Iddir because of Stigma and Discrimination as a pie chart shows below.

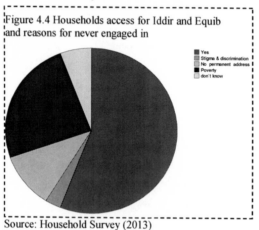

Figure 4.4 Households access for Iddir and Equib and reasons for never engaged in

Source: Household Survey (2013)

These household heads were also asked whether they have Equib (Voluntary informal revolving saving and loan group), 80(78.4%) have reported that they have no Equib and only 22(21.6%) have Equib. 72.5% respondents also reported that

110

they have no Equib because of low income 4.9% have no Equib because they have no permanent residence as a pie chart presented in front. Number of households who have no Iddir (44.1%) and Equib (78.4%) are significantly high. This clearly shows that most HIV/AIDS affected households have no strong social capital and are not in a position of sense of trust and reciprocity in the community where they are living in.

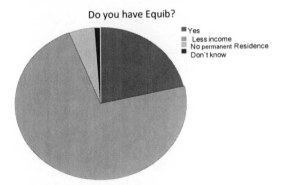

Source: Household Survey (2013)

4.6 Food Security

4.6.1 Food Consumption Score

Many people think that a problem of food insecurity is a challenge only for rural households but the problem is grater in urban households too where day to day life is more sophisticated and monetized. Given the time required to collect detailed food calorie intake at the household level, the researcher has been using what is called the Food Consumption Score as a proxy indicator of household food security which is developed by WFP. This score is calculated using information on dietary diversity (the different food items consumed by household members) and the frequencies of consumption. In this study, a composite score of the dietary diversity and food frequency has been calculated for affected households.

Households were asked to recall the type of food items their members ate over the seven days prior to the survey as well as to indicate the number of days the food type was consumed. The items consumed were grouped into food groups (staples, pulses, vegetables, fruit, meat and fish, sugar, milk, oil). These different food groups were given weights, animal proteins with the highest weight. The consumption score is calculated by summing all consumption frequencies of food items from the same group; the sum of values, after recoded, is multiplied by the respective weight for the food group.

The weighted food group scores are summed, which gives us the food consumption score (FCS). These scores are regrouped into categories using thresholds, <14 as very poor consumption, 14-21 poor consumption and so on. As table 4.19 shows below

68(66.6%) households have very poor and poor consumption score, 31(30.3%) households have average consumption and only 3(2.94%) households have good consumption score. This indicates that most HIV/AIDS infected and affected households are suffering from poor food consumption and are food insecure.

Table4. 19 Percent Distribution of households by Consumption Score Categories

Food consumption Indicator	Score	N	Percentage(%)
Very poor consumption	< 14	12	11.76
Poor consumption	14 - 21	56	55
Average/boarder line consumption	22 - 35	31	30.3
Good consumption	> 35	3	2.94
Total		102	100

Source: Household Survey (2013)

4.6.2 Food Consumption Related Negative Coping Strategies

The results of the logistic regression analysis for the three dependent variables: reducing the number of meals per day, reducing the quantity of food eaten, and skipping the entire day without eating is presented in table 20. Households headed by widowed and divorced men /women have 1.51 and 5.49 times more likelihood of employing reduction in the quantity of food the household members eat, respectively, when compared with households headed by married men/women.

113

With regard to the likelihood of applying skipping the entire day without eating as a coping strategy, it is significantly higher among widowed (OR=1.94), divorced (OR=2.15) and never married (OR=9.39), compared to households headed by married men/women. HIV/AIDS affected (ART) status of the surveyed households consistently suggested statistically significant association with the likelihood of employing all the three consumption related coping mechanisms.

As clearly demonstrated by the logistic regression results, HIV/AIDS affected Widowed and Divorced households are more likely to utilize reduction in the number of meals eaten per day, reduction in the quantity of food the household members eat, and skipping the entire day without eating, respectively, compared to Married households. PLHIV belonging to households practicing these consumption related coping strategies are less likely to escape from the practice since there is overall shortage of food in the household. While these coping strategies may be relatively effective in the absence of HIV/AIDS, the distinct nature of the disease may render them ineffective and even destructive. Contrary to the situation on the ground, to mitigate the effect of HIV/AIDS, PLHIV are encouraged to:

• Eat small and frequent meal

- Increase their energy (kilocalorie) intake by 10-30 % according to their stage compared to healthy individuals. (FANTA, 2004; WFP/WHO, 2007)

The implication of this finding is that households that are affected by HIV/AIDS are more vulnerable to practice risky coping strategies that accelerate the pace of progressing the disease to AIDS stage and finally to death among PLHIV. Due to lack of access to adequate quantity and variety of food among HIV/AIDS affected households to mitigate its impacts, the prevalence of such coping strategies may lead HIV/AIDS affected household members to adopt behaviors and livelihood strategies that put them at greater risk of HIV infection like resorting to commercial sex work or as migrant laborer to earn money for food and basic necessities.

Age group of the household head emerged as a significant predictor of exercising reduction of meal per day and skipping the entire day without eating. The result suggests that households headed by men/women in the age group 26-59 have the likelihood of employing reduction of number of meals and skipping the entire day without eating, compared to the households headed by men/women in the under 26 and over 59 age 48 ranges. These mid-span ages are where the prevalence of

HIV is highest. And most of the household members are likely to be young children. For example, according to FHI (2010) lion's share proportion of the adult HIV prevalence concentrates around the age range of 25 to 44.

The overlapping of the two variables, HIV/AIDS and food insecurity, suggests that PLHIV and small children have higher probability of being exposed to the hazards of malnutrition, poor health, and school drop-out, etc. households headed by men / women with primary and secondary and above education have 52.7 percent and 33.7 percent lower likelihood of employing skipping the entire day without eating compared to households headed by illiterate /never attended formal education, respectively. Compared to households that did not have any chronically ill member in the previous 12 months before the survey, the likelihood of practicing all the three consumption related coping strategies is higher among households who had at least one chronically ill member in the same period (significant at 1% level).

The magnitude is even higher among households who had at least one deceased adult member compared to their counterparts that did not have deceased adult member. The association of chronic illness and adult death with the risk of employing consumption related coping strategies clearly emerged from the analysis regardless of the fact that the cause of illness or death is HIV/AIDS or not.

4.5.3 Asset Disposal Related Coping Strategies

Asset disposal is another aspect of coping strategies that have negative consequences on the households. Sale of asset especially that of productive assets usually happens after exhausting consumption related coping strategies. At the first stage of asset disposal, the households dispose non-productive asset like jewelry and some household articles. When the situation is getting worse, they would resort to sale of productive asset like land and house. Sometimes it is tricky to identify such measures as "coping" since they render households more insecure and vulnerable in the long run.

In this sub-section, two coping strategies related to asset disposal are selected for analysis to examine their correlates among the surveyed households. Logistic regression coefficients and their odds ratios are estimated for 1) selling household articles, jewelry, and furniture and 2) selling/renting fixed assets (land, Electronics, house, etc). In both models, the

117

dependent variable is zero/one dummy variable identifying households that employed the coping strategies using the data. The independent variables include demographic and educational, sickness, mortality, food support, housing, etc.

As it has been the case in the consumption related coping strategies, clear picture of association emerged between HIV/AIDS affected status (on ART) of the households and practicing of the two asset disposal coping strategies. This may be explained by the fact that HIV/AIDS affected households tend more to sell/rent their asset to cope with the negative consequences of AIDS shock. Specifically, sale of productive assets usually happen when it is absolutely necessary for survival. On the other hand, HIV/AIDS affected (on ART) households may be forced to sell/rent out assets like land, house equipments etc. because of shortage of labor.

As implied by level of significance (significant at 1 % level) and magnitude of the odds ratio, the type of house the household possessed is an important predictor of selling household asset. Possession of rented from private and kebele houses increases the likelihood of selling household articles, jewelry, and furniture by 5.5 and 8 times, respectively, compared to households possessing own house. The result of the second model, selling /renting out fixed asset, is not statistically significant to the type of house the household possessed. Thus, sale/renting out of fixed assets like land is less likely to be determined by the type of house possessed by the household. Households that have experienced adult chronic illness and death in the previous 12 months before the survey are more likely to exercise both asset disposal coping strategies. This holds true regardless of the chronic illness or death. The magnitudes of the odds ratios for the per capita of the quantity of food from own purchase and other food support sources are very small. Thus, the effect of these two variables on the likelihood of practicing the two coping strategies does not seem to be substantial.

CHAPTER 5: CONCLUSIONS AND RECOMMENDATIONS

5.1 Conclusions

The study has examined the effects of HIV/AIDS on urban livelihood and food security through investigating effects on human, physical, financial and social capital as well as examining food consumption and coping strategies. From descriptive and multivariate analysis which controls for other factors while analyzing the effects of HIV/AIDS, the researcher has seen that HIV/AIDS has affected all the four forms of capital and has contributed to food insecurity. Households have to struggle with food shortages caused by inadequate income, poor housing and hygiene access, high costs of medication and loss of employment, high socioeconomic information gap and so on

The study results show many deaths and cases of chronic illness among affected households. As many as 18 deaths were reported over a 12 months period prior to the survey. As a result of a higher number of deaths and chronic illness, HIV/AIDS affected households showed a much different household structure such as a higher number of widows and widowers, a higher dependency, a much higher number of (single) orphans. There is a much higher percentage of FHH affected and have fared badly on many of the indicators used for analysis.

Household heads or their spouses constitute a substantial proportion of the deceased and chronically ill. Household heads and spouses are usually the primary bread winners of households. The loss of these core members due to AIDS causes an increase in number of orphans and leads to loss of accumulated knowledge which is normally transferred to succeeding generations. Loss of knowledge will consequently reduce the labor productivity in the economy.

Regarding the effects of HIV/AIDS on household assets, a higher proportion of households reported selling productive assets in order to meet health and funeral costs. Erosion of assets is a serious blow to HIV affected households as the livelihood strategy is pinned upon formation of capital. Concerning financial capital, the income and saving of households is too meager to sustain life. On the other hand some households borrowed money for small business activities which is a good sign of recovery that must be strengthened.

When it comes to food security status, households affected by HIV/AIDS had poor consumption which is revealed both by the consumption score which combined frequency of meals with diversity and the finding that more affected households had used negative consumption related coping strategies, like skipping meals, which undermine their nutrition and remain food insecure.

5.2 Recommendations

Implementation of the selected recommendations below will first of all require multidisciplinary approach to make them operational. It will also require careful thinking on targeting households affected by HIV/AIDS so that they will not face stigma and all its related consequences such as dependency on aid syndrome.

The overall approach to address the effects of HIV/AIDS on urban livelihoods should be, for government and non government agencies as well as communities, business men and other concerned bodies to meaningful and committed incorporation of HIV/AIDS issues into their core business. This will require analyzing not only the effects of HIV/AIDS but how a program can best address the effects. The specific measures that can be taken within an overall approach of integration with core development policies and activities include the following.

Often a large proportion of the urban poor are forced to work in the informal sector, earning low incomes for long hours of work. Competition for work is intense, usually making incomes very low. For such workers, insurance, health care or sick pay do not exist. In addition, informal sectors are often associated with a non-dependable stream of income and precarious working conditions. Working in poor conditions serves to increase long-term vulnerability to disease and ill health.

☞ Therefore, government and non-government stakeholders can work together and crate viable job opportunities for these HIV affected poor and illiterate households such as government can provide land for production and marketing while non-government organizations can provide trainings and working capital.

☞ Government can set agreement with private informal and formal sectors about minimum wages they have to pay and working conditions that may further complicates the health of HIV affected households.

☞ Non- governmental organizations can provide life skill, psychosocial, on job and pre job trainings for poor and illiterate adult PLHIVs so as to enable them contribute effective labor.

☞ Positive living, small income generating activities business development, recording, documentation trainings can capacitate PLHIVs to cope the urban dynamic life and able to generate sustainable income that improves their households' livelihood.

School support can be given to households whose children are absent from school.

▸ The appropriate form of school support needs to be worked out depending on the reason why the children are not going to school and depending on what form of assistance already exists.

▸ Adult trainings can also improve and capacitate household heads.

▸ Non-governmental organizations and government stakeholders can provide psychosocial support and counseling service on the issues such as marriage, positive living, tolerance and trust etc. for widowed and divorced household heads especially and for the affected people generally.

Loss of knowledge/skills: Small and micro institutions agency should target households who have lost knowledge/skills through death of an adult. Micro enterprises need to be women/youth friendly. Training of Micro enterprises workers on the effects HIV/AIDS has on households' income and able to labor work specifically and on urban livelihoods in general is very crucial.

Poor food consumption: In order to address the poor consumption experienced, particularly by PLHIV, the following measures can be taken:

▶ Diversifying income/food from less labor intensive activities. Assistance could be given to these households to raise highly nutritious products like poultry, vegetables (home gardens) and small ruminants.

▶ When the resource is available, free food/cash assistance should be provided in dependency minimizing/discouraging manner.

▶ The training of the health extension workers should include nutritional counseling to PLHIV so that they can assist in applying the appropriate dietary and nutrition related practices to mitigate the effects of the illness and medication.

▶ Trainings how to prepare nutritious food from locally available food sources can be provided.

Asset protection: in order to support households who deplete their assets to buy food, medicine or pay for funeral costs, the measures mentioned above in terms of direct food/cash support or credit for income generating activities will be appropriate. The credit need to be more flexible and tailor made to households affected by HIV/AIDS who may face labor shortage to work and pay back within a specified time frame.

☞ Kebele administrators can give priority to provide house for poor PLHIVs

☞ Government housing programs shall take due consideration for these poor vulnerable PLHIVs.

☞ Business organizations, non-governmental organizations and the government sector employers can set priority to favor poor PLHIVs during labor recruitments so that to reduce further asset depletion.

☞ Generally, to combat HIV/AIDS and to mitigate its effects and impacts on the already impoverished households; multispectral functioning, resource coordination, involvement of PLHIVs during problem identification, planning and implementation, target focused, empowerment (women and girls), community participation are the key basic elements that HIV focused works are still lacking and needs to be given due attention.

☞ Above all, creating employment opportunity for these poor, desperate and prone HIV/AIDS infected and affected households in urban areas can play vital role for sustainable livelihood transformation and hence food security as well as combating the effects and impacts of the disease.

BIBLIOGRAPHY

AVERT .ORG (2009).The Impact of HIV & AIDS on Africa.
Barnett, T. (2001). The Social and economic impact of HIV/AIDS
in poor countries: a review of studies and lessons, Progress in
Development Studies 1, 2(2001) pp.151-170.

Alemtsehay and Tsegazeab (2008), The Impacts of HIV/AIDS on
Livelihoods and Food Security in Rural Ethiopia: Results from
household Survey in Four Regions, United Nations World Food
Program.

Amhara regional HAPCO (2012), Regional progress report,
presented on regional HIV/TB annual submit

Bahir Dar City HAPCO (2012), Annual progress report, presented
on City HIV/AIDS council meeting.

Barnett, T. and Whiteside, A.(2000). Guidelines for Studies of the
Social and Economic Impact of HIV/AIDS, UNAIDS, Geneva

Baylies, C. (2002). The Impact of AIDS on Rural Households in
Africa: A Shock Like Any Other? Development and Change
33(4):611-632 (2002).Institute of Social Studies, Blackwell
Publishers UK.

Bollinger, L., Stover, J., and Seyoum, E., (1999). The Economic Impact of AIDS in Ethiopia; The Future Group International in Collaboration with: Research Triangle Institute (RTI), The Center for Development and Population Activities (CEDPA).

Booysen, F., Rensburg D. Van, Bachmann, M., Engelbeecht, M. and Steyn F.(2001).The socio-economic impact of HIV-AIDS on households in South Africa Medical Research Council of South Africa, South Africa.

Care international (2010), Women and HIV/AIDS, an International Resource Book, Information, action and resources on Women and HIV/AIDS, reproductive health and sexual relationships, Pundera Press, London.
Common Wealth Secretariat (2002), Gender and Development in socioeconomic perspectives of least developing countries: Blackwell Publishers UK.

Demele, H. (2004). Socioeconomic Consequences of HIV and AIDS for HIV-positive Women in Addis Ababa and their Coping Strategies. MA Thesis, Addis Ababa University, Economic Commission for Africa /ECA/ (2003) Africa: The Socio-Economic Impact of HIV/AIDS. Commission on HIV/AIDS and Governance in Africa URL: www.uneca.org

Emmanuel, N. and Carole, R. (2005) Urban Families Under Presser. Birmingham University

Family Health International (FHI) Ethiopia in Collaboration with Addis Ababa City   Administration Health Bureau (2002) Addis Ababa HIV Care and Support Service
Assessment, August 2002.

Federica Marzo (2004) The Impact of HIV/AIDS on Chronic and Transient Poverty. First draft March 2004. Université de Paris 1 and CNRS.MSE 106-112 Bd de l.Hôpital 75647 Paris Cedex 13. federica.marzo@malix.univ.paris1.fr

FHI (2011), Mapping and Census of Female Sex Workers in Addis Ababa, Ethiopia
Addis Ababa.

Fenton, L., (2004).   Preventing HIV/AIDS through poverty reduction; the only sustainable solution. International Health and Medical Education Center, University College London   in WWW.thelanct.com vol. 364 pp. 1186-87 September 25, 2004 state of world population
Impact of HIV/AIDS on Poverty at Household level: The case of Addis Ababa

Garbus, L., (2003).HIV/AIDS in Ethiopia, AIDS Policy Research Center, University of California.

Gow, J., and Desmond, C., (2002). Impacts and Interventions: The HIV/AIDS Epidemic and the Children of South Africa. UNCEF, University of Natal Press. IRIN NEWS.ORG (2004) Ethiopia: New Project launched to help HIV/AIDS affected families.

Israel, Glen D. (1992).Determining Sample Size, Program Evaluation and Organization development, IFAS, University of Florida. PEOD-6

James, K. (2004). HIV/AIDS and the Changing Role of the Aged Understanding the Role, Constraints and Consequences for the elderly as providers of education to children orphaned by HIV/AIDS, School of education, Makerere University, Uganda.

Ministry of Finance and Economic Development /MoFED/ (2002) Ethiopia: Sustainable Development and Poverty Reduction Program. July 2002. Impact of HIV/AIDS on Poverty at Household level: The case of Addis Ababa

Ministry of Health (MoH), (2009/10). Health and Health Related Indicators, Planning and Programming Department, MoH.

MOLSA, Italian Cooperation, and UNICEF (2009). Survey on the Prevalence and Characteristics of AIDS Orphans in Ethiopia, Children, Youth and Family Affairs Department, Ministry of Labor and Social Affairs (MOLSA), February 2009, Addis Ababa.

Moser, C. (1998). The Asset Vulnerability Framework: Reassessing Urban Poverty Reduction Strategies. World Development, Vol. 26, No. 1, pp. l-19.

Mukiza-Gapere, J., and J.P. M. Ntozi (1995). Impacts of AIDS on the family and mortality in Uganda. Health Transition Review, Supplement to volume 5, 1995, 191-200.

Pankhurst, A., (2004). Conceptions of and responses to HIV/AIDS: Views from Twenty Ethiopian Rural Villages, Department of Sociology and Anthropology, Addis Ababa University.

Philipos Petros (2002). The Impact of AIDS Orphans on Development: The Case of Addis Ababa, MA Thesis, Addis Ababa University.

Potsiou, C. (2010). Rapid Urbanization and Mega Cities: The Need for Spatial Information Management. International Federation of Surveyors (FIG) Publication No 48, Copenhagen, Denmark

Quarantelli, E. (ND). Urban Vulnerability to Disasters in Developing Countries: Managing Risks thematic overview of Urban: Blackwell Publishers UK.

Richter, L., Manegold, J., and Pather, R. (2004). Family and Community Interventions for Children Affected by AIDS, Human Sciences Research Council, Cape Town, South Africa.

Thomas, S. (2008). Urbanization as a driver of change, The Arup Journal, No. 1/2008.

UNAIDS (2012), Report on the Global HIV/AIDS Epidemic, UNAIDS.

UNDP (2012), Human Development Report 2011, Oxford: University Press.

UNFPA (2011), People, Poverty and Possibilities, UNFPA
UNICEF (2009), Country progress reports on HIV/AIDs orphans and vulnerabilities, UNICEF

USAID (2012), HIV/AIDS risk and vulnerability of poor countries of the world, USAID

WFP, VAM: Draft Food Consumption Analysis: Calculation and use of Food Consumption Score in Food Consumption Analysis.